Developing

Inner Strength

BY

Charles F. Stanley

Thomas Nelson
Since 1798

Developing Inner Strength

Charles F. Stanley

Copyright © 1998, 2008 by Charles F. Stanley

Published in Nashville, Tennessee, by Thomas Nelson, Inc.

Scripture references are from the NEW KING JAMES VERSION of the Bible. Copyright © 1979, 1980, 1982, Thomas Nelson, Inc., Publishers.

Editing, layout, and design by Gregory C. Benoit Publishing, Old Mystic, CT

ISBN 978-1-4185-2815-7

Printed in the United States of America

08 09 10 11 12 RRD 5 4 3 2 1

Contents

INTRODUCTION
The Hope of Greater Strength..1

LESSON 1
Receiving God's Gift of Inner Strength.................................3

LESSON 2
Strength in Times of Loneliness..9

LESSON 3
Strength in Times of Fear...21

LESSON 4
Strength in Times of Abuse..36

LESSON 5
Strength in Times of Criticism...48

LESSON 6
Strength in Times of Guilt..59

LESSON 7
Strength in Times of Frustration...71

LESSON 8
Strength in Times of Burnout...85

LESSON 9
Strength in Times of Persecution...98

LESSON 10
Strength in Times of Brokenness.......................................114

INTRODUCTION

The Hope of Greater Strength

A great deal has been written in recent years about inner healing, emotional wounds, and reversing low self-esteem. Bookstores are lined with self-help books. What so many people in our world do not realize is that the Bible has been the authoritative book on the healing and strengthening of the human soul (mind, emotions, will) for thousands of years. The Bible is not a self-help book but a God-will-help book. The Bible holds out the hope and promise of God's eternal help for the person who humbly turns to Him.

When times of emotional pain or weakness come, we eventually reach the end of ourselves. There are those who teach that turning to God is a sign of emotional weakness, but the exact opposite is true. No person can fully heal his own spirit, soul, or body. Certain problems and conditions lie beyond a person's *capacity* to self-heal.

The good news for the Christian is that the end of self is often the beginning for God! The help that God offers us in His Word is both eternal and timely. It is highly effective and freely available to all. I encourage you to keep your Bible close at hand as we move through this ten-part study. Make notes in the margins as you look up various Scriptures and study them. It is far more important that you write God's insights into the Bible than to write in this book, although places are provided here for you to make notes.

This book can be used by you alone or by several people in a small-group study. At various times, you will be asked to relate to the material in one of these four ways:

1

1. *What new insights have you gained?* Make notes about the insights that you have. You may want to record them in your Bible or in a separate journal. As you reflect back over your insights, you are likely to see how God has moved in your life.

2. *Have you ever had a similar experience?* Each of us approaches the Bible from a unique background—our own particular set of relationships and experiences. Our experiences do not make the Bible true—the Word of God is truth regardless of our opinion about it. It is important, however, to share our experiences in order to see how God's truth can be applied to human lives.

3. *How do you feel about the material presented?* Emotional responses do not give validity to the Scriptures, nor should we trust our emotions as a gauge for our faith. In small-group Bible study, however, it is good for participants to express their emotions. The Holy Spirit often communicates with us through this unspoken language.

4. *In what way do you feel challenged to respond or to act?* God's Word may cause you to feel inspired or challenged to change something in your life. Take the challenge seriously and find ways of acting upon it. If God reveals to you a particular need that He wants *you* to address, take that as "marching orders" from God. God is expecting you to *do* something with the challenge that He has just given you.

Start and conclude your Bible study sessions in prayer. Ask God to give you spiritual eyes to see and spiritual ears to hear. As you conclude your study, ask the Lord to seal what you have learned so that you will never forget it. Ask Him to help you grow into the fullness of the stature of Christ Jesus.

Again, I caution you to keep the Bible at the center of your study. A genuine Bible study stays focused on God's Word and promotes a growing faith and a closer walk with the Holy Spirit in *each* person who participates.

LESSON 1

Receiving God's Gift of Inner Strength

ᕦ In This Lesson ᕤ

LEARNING: HOW CAN I GET RID OF MY EMOTIONAL BAGGAGE?

GROWING: WHAT PART DOES GOD PLAY IN THIS, AND WHAT PART DO I PLAY?

ᕦ᛫ᕤ

Jesus said in Luke 4:18:

> The Spirit of the LORD is upon Me,
> Because He has anointed Me
> To preach the gospel to the poor;
> He has sent Me to heal the brokenhearted,
> To proclaim liberty to the captives
> And recovery of sight to the blind,
> To set at liberty those who are oppressed.

Jesus came to this earth to take care of our sin problem and to make it possible for us to experience forgiveness and eternal life. He also came to make us whole from the inside out. With wholeness comes emotional, mental, and spiritual strength.

The Holy Spirit is God's gift to us, that we might become more and more like Jesus and experience what He purchased for us on the cross in an ever deepening, ever more potent way. No matter who we are today, we are "poor" in some way. We each lack something or are a little weaker in one area of our emotional makeup than in other areas. No person is 100 percent strong in all areas of his life at all times. Just as we are healthier physically on some days than on others, so we go through periods when we experience a weakness in our emotions.

When those times of emotional weakness come, we generally experience emotional pain. If we deal with our emotional pain as soon as it arises, receiving God's help and healing for the injury that we have suffered, this pain is generally temporary. At other times, however, the emotional pain lingers. We may not deal with it, hoping that it will go away or heal itself. We may not know how to deal with the pain, and continue to struggle on without relief. We may not believe that we should deal with the pain, thinking perhaps that pain is inevitable and a normal part of every person's life.

If you are experiencing emotional pain today, I have three thoughts:

1. Time will not heal your pain, but Jesus Christ can and will heal you in your emotions if you turn to Him and receive the strength that He offers to you.

2. The Bible presents God's ways for dealing with emotional pain; you must learn what the Bible says and apply God's truth to your life.

3. God wants you to live in emotional freedom and strength, unshackled by emotional weakness or inner pain.

The results of an ongoing, lingering emotional pain that goes unaddressed and unhealed can be devastating to a person and to a family. Lingering or pervasive emotional weakness saps a person's energy, drains away creativity, diverts the person's motivation and enthusiasm for life, and affects his relationships. If left unhealed, it can even cause serious damage to the person's physical health and to overall effectiveness as a witness for Christ in this world.

None of these conditions are God's desire for you! Rather, God desires that you be filled with a vitality and enthusiasm for life, be creative in every area of talent and skill that He has given, have healthy and vibrant relationships, and be an effective witness to the gospel of Jesus Christ.

Let me ask you several questions:

∽ Are you lonely?

∽ Do you feel restless and frustrated?

∽ Is anxiety eating away at your joy?

∽ Do you feel burned out, insecure, broken—as if you are a failure?

These conditions are all symptoms of emotional wounds that weaken us and make us more vulnerable to manipulation and injury by other people, and also to attacks in the spiritual realm. These are the very symptoms that Jesus came to heal and to strengthen. He said that He came to:

∽ heal the brokenhearted

∽ proclaim liberty to the captives

∽ bring sight to the blind

∽ set at liberty those who are oppressed

5

Emotional pain and weakness cause us to feel dejected, "bound up" on the inside, blind to the goodness of God, and imprisoned in our own darkness. Jesus came to set us free and to make us whole; He came to impart to us a deep, abiding, and consistent strength, and then to develop His strength within us.

Our Part in the Process

Jesus is the Savior, the Healer, the Deliverer, the One who makes us whole. There is a twofold role, however, that we are required to play in bringing about healing of our emotions and receiving God's strength.

∽ Emotional Baggage ∽

1. *We must be willing to set down our emotional baggage.* Emotional baggage is a term that refers to old feelings, thought patterns, and past experiences that continue to traumatize a person every time they are triggered or recalled. Some people have become so accustomed to carrying heavy emotional baggage that they can't imagine life without that burden. They are so familiar with emotional pain that they can't imagine life without pain. In fact, the thought of letting go of something in their past is threatening to them.

In some cases, a person may feel that he is opening himself up to increased vulnerability or greater accountability—which may be true. But what is not true is that greater vulnerability or accountability automatically leads to renewed pain. Jesus can be present in any situation to comfort, love, and nurture us when we make ourselves vulnerable to Him and open up our lives to receive the fullness of His love and forgiveness. Jesus is present whenever we face up to our sin and make amends; He helps us to become accountable to Him and to others, always in a framework of love and forgiveness.

There is no benefit in continuing to carry emotional burdens. There is no good reason for hanging on to what slows you down, keeps you from being vibrantly alive and strong, or stops you from experiencing the fullness of life that God has prepared for you. On the other hand, there is every good reason to set down your emotional baggage at the foot of the cross and to walk forward in your life with a new freedom to your step!

Today is a great day for coming to the Lord and saying, "Lord Jesus, I am at the end of my ability to heal my own emotions. I cannot make myself strong. I lay down my emotional burdens, pain, and weakness at Your feet, and with Your help I resolve never to pick them up again."

∞ Let the Lord do His Part ∞

2. *We must invite the Lord to do His work in our lives.* The Holy Spirit will not overstep the boundaries of your own will. God will not invade your life and strip away from you your painful memories or heal your withered emotions unless you ask Him to do this work in you. Today is a great day for asking the Lord Jesus to take from your heart the emotional load that you are carrying, to heal your emotional wounds, to bind up your emotional pain, and to set you free from emotional bondage. Invite Him to begin a healing work within you: "Lord Jesus, I ask You to heal me and make me strong in emotions, mind, and will. Please give me the courage to walk through life without the pain, insecurities, frustrations, and alienation that I have been feeling. I trust You to set me free, make me whole, and keep me strong."

Today is a day for new beginnings toward a stronger tomorrow!

❧ What new insights do you hope to gain through this study?

❧ In what areas have you struggled with emotional pain or injury in the past? When have you felt the need for greater inner strength?

❧ Are you open to God's healing of hurtful memories?

❧ Today and Tomorrow: ❧

TODAY: GOD WANTS ME TO BE FREE OF ALL MY EMOTIONAL BAGGAGE.

TOMORROW: I WILL PRAYERFULLY SEEK GOD'S HELP IN LETTING GO OF MY
    BAGGAGE.

LESSON 2

Strength in Times of Loneliness

❧ In This Lesson: ☙

LEARNING: WHAT CAN I DO TO NOT FEEL SO LONELY?

GROWING: HOW CAN I GAIN MORE FRIENDS?

I have met hundreds—even thousands—of people through the years who have felt utterly alone, abandoned, ostracized, and lonely. Loneliness is one of the most excruciating feelings that nearly every person attempts to avoid at all costs. Even so, loneliness seems pervasive in our world today. Older people frequently express their loneliness, especially after the death of a spouse.

Divorced people feel lonely. Young people often think that they are totally alone in their feelings, especially if they have indifferent, self-absorbed parents. Salesmen on the road are lonely. Mothers who stay at home all day with young children often speak of loneliness. Those who have empty nests are lonely. Newly retired persons, accustomed to a wide circle of colleagues, are lonely. Loneliness abounds.

The Bible begins (Genesis 1 through 3) with a picture of the fellowship that God desires with human beings. He said, "Let Us make man in Our image, according to Our likeness" (Genesis 1:26). God displays a desire for companionship. Loneliness is not a desirable state, from God's point of view. Adam walked and talked with God frequently. His voice

9

in the cool of the evening was not strange to him (see Genesis 3:8–9).

Throughout the Old Testament we find the Lord reaching out to His people, revealing Himself to them, desiring to be with them and to communicate with them. In 1 Samuel 12:22 we find this promise of God: "For the LORD will not forsake His people, for His great name's sake, because it has pleased the LORD to make you His people."

Jesus Experienced Both Loneliness and Friendship

In the New Testament, we read how Jesus developed a very close relationship with His disciples. He was so concerned that they continue in their relationship with one another even after His crucifixion that He spent much of His last night with them talking about their need to remain with one another, and to be as one with the Father. Jesus says in the Gospel of John:

> "Let not your heart be troubled; you believe in God, believe also in Me. In My Father's house are many mansions; if it were not so, I would have told you. I go to prepare a place for you. And if I go and prepare a place for you, I will come again and receive you to Myself; that where I am, there you may be also."

> —John 14:1–3

> "I will pray the Father, and He will give you another Helper, that He may abide with you forever—the Spirit of truth, whom the world cannot receive, because it neither sees Him nor knows Him; but you know Him, for He dwells with you and will be in you. I will not leave you orphans; I will come to you."

> —John 14:16–18

"As the Father loved Me, I also have loved you; abide in My love."

—John 15:9

"This is My commandment, that you love one another as I have loved you. Greater love has no one than this, than to lay down one's life for his friends."

—John 15:12–13

How do these verses relate to loneliness?

Note that most of these verses deal with our relationship with God. What does this suggest about dealing with loneliness?

The close communion that the Lord desires is something that we can count on, even if everyone else abandons us. Jesus knew this to be true in His own life. On the night that He was arrested and tried, He said to His disciples, "Indeed the hour is coming, yes, has now come, that you will be scattered, each to his own, and will leave Me alone." Can you hear the pain in that statement? Jesus knew what it was to be lonely. But then Jesus went on to say, "And yet I am not alone, because the Father is with Me" (John 16:32). Jesus knew what it was to be comforted even in the face of abandonment.

The good news for every Christian is that Jesus is our Friend of friends. He is with us always and He never changes, abandons us, or withdraws from us. We can trust Him always to be present so that we never are truly alone.

⁓ What insight do you gain from the fact that Jesus experienced loneliness?

"...and lo, I am with you always, even to the end of the age."

—Matthew 28:20

☙ In what way is Jesus "with you always"? If He is not physically present, what does this verse mean?

∞ Feeling Alone versus Being Alone ∞

Being alone is a blessing to some people who find themselves continually surrounded by people. For others, being alone brings about great feelings of loneliness. For still others, loneliness is so pervasive in their souls that they can feel lonely even in a room full of people.

You must continually guard your mind against the idea that you are an isolated example or one-of-a-kind in your feelings of loneliness. The truth is that you are *never* alone: the Holy Spirit is present and available to you always, and there are many other Christian people who have experienced what you are experiencing and who would *like* to be a friend to you. At times when we are lonely we simply need to reach out to others and invite their presence into our lives.

The prophet Elijah once felt very isolated and alone. He cried out to God, "The children of Israel have forsaken Your covenant, torn down Your altars, and killed Your prophets with the sword. I alone am left; and they seek to take my life" (1 Kings 19:14). Can you hear the desperation and loneliness in Elijah's words? Not only did he feel forsaken, but he felt that all of Israel had forsaken the things that were most important to him.

The Lord responded to Elijah, "Go, return on your way to the Wilderness of Damascus ... Yet I have reserved seven thousand in Israel, all whose knees have not bowed to Baal, and every mouth that has not kissed him" (1 Kings 19:15, 18). Elijah was not truly alone as a follower of the Lord God and a keeper of God's covenant—and there were 7,000 people with whom he might associate!

The same is likely to be true for you. You are not alone, and there are more people who feel as you feel and believe as you believe than you presently know! Seek them out.

Read 1 Kings 19:1–18.

What factors might have contributed to Elijah's feelings of loneliness in this passage?

๛ What things did God do for Elijah to help his loneliness? Why did he still feel discouraged?

What to Do When You Feel Lonely

You simply cannot be alone once you have the Spirit of God dwelling in you. Even so, you can have a *feeling* of being alone even if you aren't alone. What, then, should you do when you have feelings of loneliness?

Lonely people turn to many things that create more loneliness, rather than to those things that can alleviate their feelings. They turn to drugs and alcohol, both of which tend to alienate and turn away the very people with whom they might enjoy companionship. They sometimes turn to television, videos, or radio programs, all of which tend to isolate a person from human-to-human communication.

The foremost antidote to feeling lonely is this: good relationships with Christian people. The Lord said, "It is not good that man should be alone"—and then He took the necessary step to resolve the situation:

"I will make him a helper comparable to him" (Genesis 2:18). We often think that this verse applies only to marriage, but it can also apply to godly friendships. The Lord's desire is that you have a close, intimate relationship with Him *and* that you have satisfying and enriching personal relationships with other people.

> A man who has friends must himself be friendly, But there is a friend who sticks closer than a brother.
>
> —Proverbs 18:24

List the traits that you desire to have in a friend.

How many of those traits do *you* have?

∞ Being Friendly ∞

Now ask yourself an even more important question, "Am I willing to *be* this kind of friend?" To have a friend, you must be a friend.

Here are just a few things that you can do to put yourself into the "market" for developing friendships:

∞ Accept invitations to social events with godly people.

∞ Get involved with your church and with various ministries within your church. Be faithful in your participation in group functions. Serving the Lord in an active way with other believers is a wonderful way for friendships to develop.

∞ Invite others to join you for lunch or after-church brunch.

∞ Participate in retreats that are sponsored by your church or by Christian organizations, especially ones that involve other people who live in your area. Getting away for a weekend or going to a seminar with other Christians is a great way to meet people who are likely to have common interests with you.

∞ Join Christian clubs or hobby groups—a men's group that engages in outdoor activities or sports, a Christian businessmen's group, an exercise class, or a Christian choir.

∞ Join a Bible study group. Studying with other Christians is a good way to make new friends who share an interest in similar topics. Sometimes community learning programs or neighborhood schools offer non-academic courses in such things as gourmet cooking, photography, or art appreciation.

Ask the Lord to reveal to you the people who may be your future friends. At the same time, ask Him to bring to your mind those friends whom you may have neglected recently; ask Him to show you ways in which you might rekindle old friendships.

Friendship is a good thing! It is God's will that you have friends. Therefore, when you ask the Lord to bring good Christian friends into your life, you are asking something that is according to God's will. Look for God to bring people your way. Look for new opportunities to arise for you to be a friend, and in the process, to gain a friend.

> Now this is the confidence that we have in Him, that if we ask anything according to His will, He hears us. And if we know that He hears us, whatever we ask, we know that we have the petitions that we have asked of Him.

> —1 John 5:14–15

What does this passage teach us about asking God for friends?

Take time right now to talk with God about your loneliness.

∞ Trusting God ∞

In all things, remember Romans 8:28: "all things work together for good to those who love God, to those who are the called according to His purpose." The good news of this verse applies to your friendships! God is the engineer of social relationships, and He has a way of bringing the right people into your life at the right times for the right purposes. Sometimes friendships last a lifetime. Sometimes they are intended only for a season of life. Trust God to bring you the friends that you need right now—and also to bring *you* to those who need *your* friendship.

Do not give up on a Christian friend because you feel that he has disappointed you, has withdrawn from you, or is in conflict with you. Ask your friend if you have done something to damage your friendship— for example, if you have made an inadvertent mistake, if you have required too much of your friendship, or if you have failed at being a good friend. If so, apologize to your friend and seek to make amends. Value your friendships enough to do your best to maintain them and develop them over time.

Keep in mind always that our own feelings sometimes deceive us. None of us have perfect perception, and especially so when we personally are involved. Ask God to help you build your life upon the truth of His Word and the consistent reliability of God's presence and power. Feelings come and go. God's love, forgiveness, and presence are eternal and rock solid.

∞ In the past, how have you met the people who became your close friends? What practical ideas can you gain for finding future friends?

For I am persuaded that neither death nor life, nor angels nor principalities nor powers, nor things present nor things to come, nor height nor depth, nor any other created thing, shall be able to separate us from the love of God which is in Christ Jesus our Lord.

—Romans 8:38-39

🐚 Go through the list of things in these verses, giving real-life examples of each.

🐚 Which of these things have you experienced in your own life? How can these verses help you find comfort?

🐚 Today and Tomorrow: 🐚

TODAY: GOD DOES NOT WANT ME TO BE ALONE ANY MORE THAN I DO.

TOMORROW: I WILL ASK THE LORD TO LEAD ME TO NEW FRIENDS THIS WEEK, AND ALSO TO THOSE WHO NEED FRIENDS.

LESSON 3

Strength in Times of Fear

—————— ❧ In This Lesson: ❧ ——————

LEARNING: WHAT IS THE ROOT CAUSE OF MY ANXIETIES?

GROWING: HOW CAN I LEARN TO TRUST GOD MORE?

My insecurities and fears as a child were no doubt linked to the fact that I had relatively few things that were consistent. We moved 17 times in the first 16 years of my life. We never really seemed to have enough, especially in my early years when my mother was struggling as a young widow to provide food and shelter for the two of us. My mother was solely responsible for an active, curious son, and this made her very protective. She frequently said to me, "Don't fall down," "Watch out," "Be careful." The message to me was one of doom and gloom: "Don't take any risks, life is scary, and you're going to get hurt."

Furthermore, I was raised with the concept that God was a stern judge, just waiting to pounce on a little boy who might step out of line. From my earliest memories, I never dreamed of doing anything bad. I was too scared of the consequences! My entire outlook on life was one of deep emotional insecurity, anxiety, and fear. It took years of living with a full understanding of God's love, tenderness, and steadfast provision for me to overcome these negative emotions.

Again, I know that I am not alone in my experience with these emotions. Everywhere I look today, I find people living anxious lives. In fact, if we had only one word to describe our society it might be *anxious*. People aren't sure whom they can count on. The world seems to be changing rapidly on all fronts. Old moral and ethical standards in our culture have fallen away dramatically in recent years. Parents, stepparents, and foster parents come and go in the lives of an increasing number of children; spouses seem more temporary than permanent in people's lives. A life in which such fluctuations and changes are the norm is nearly always an *anxious* life.

~ When have you experienced times of anxiety or fear?

~ Do you live with a pervasive feeling of anxiety? What might be the root causes for this feeling?

The Root of Anxiety

Anxiety is fear of the future. We feel anxious when we come to the conclusion that the future holds no promise of change or when we aren't sure what's going to happen from one moment to the next. Sometimes anxiety is rooted in a person's feelings that he is incapable of handling a new challenge. At other times, anxiety is rooted in setting standards that are too high, even impossible. Sometimes anxiety is rooted in a person's feeling torn between two opinions or between two people. At times, anxiety is rooted in unresolved hostility.

Jesus knew all about these causes of anxiety. Anxiety over life's basic needs was a problem when He walked the earth. Jesus lived in an area that was occupied by Rome, and nobody was ever sure what Rome might do next or what new taxes and laws might be issued against the Jews. Daily life was difficult: thousands upon thousands lived a hand-to-mouth, day-to-day existence. Sickness and disease were prevalent. Great tension existed between those who considered themselves to be "Law-keeping" Jews and those who were perceived to be Law-breakers.

This is what Jesus taught His disciples in Luke 12:22–30:

> Therefore I say to you, do not worry about your life, what you will eat; nor about the body, what you will put on. Life is more than food, and the body is more than clothing. Consider the ravens, for they neither sow nor reap, which have neither storehouse nor barn; and God feeds them. Of how much more value are you than the birds? And which of you by worrying can add one cubit to his stature? If you then are not able to do the least, why are you anxious for the rest? Consider the lilies, how they grow: they neither toil nor spin; and yet I say to you, even Solomon in all his glory was not arrayed like one

of these. If then God so clothes the grass, which today is in the field and tomorrow is thrown into the oven, how much more will He clothe you, O you of little faith? And do not seek what you should eat or what you should drink, nor have an anxious mind. For all these things the nations of the world seek after, and your Father knows that you need these things.

∾ What root causes of anxiety does Jesus address in these verses? Which ones apply to your own life?

∾ How much more valuable are you in God's eyes than birds? Consider the price that He paid for your salvation. How does this affect your own areas of anxiety?

As you look at Jesus' teachings about anxiety, note these three things:

1. *God knows what you need.* Much of our anxiety is rooted in a feeling that we must maintain control over every detail in our lives because there is nobody else whom we can trust to know our needs and to provide for us. Jesus made it very clear, "Your Father knows." He knows because He cares for us with an infinite love. We are of exceedingly great value to Him.

2. *God will supply what you need.* God knows what you need, and He knows by what means, when, and precisely how much to supply you so that your need is met fully. He is a loving Father who desires the best for His children, which includes a full provision.

3. *Only God can alleviate your feelings of anxiety.* Nobody else can ever fully know or meet this need in your life. God alone sees the beginning from the ending of your life, and He alone knows what you will need at precisely every moment of your life in order for you to do the work and fulfill the plan that He has for you.

God provides for us *as we trust Him.* His part is to meet our needs. Our part is to *trust* Him to meet our needs.

> But seek the kingdom of God, and all these things shall be added to you.
>
> —Luke 12:31

∽ What does it mean to "seek the kingdom of God"? Give practical examples.

∽ Why does Jesus promise that the things listed in the previous verses "shall be added to you"? Why didn't He say that we would **acquire** those things?

The Need for a Personal Relationship with Christ

The first and foremost step to overcoming anxiety is to make certain that you have a personal relationship with Jesus Christ. To do that, you need to come sincerely and honestly to God and say, "I want to have a relationship with You. I accept what You have done for me—that You have sent Jesus Christ to this earth to die in my place and to be the sacrifice for my sins. I accept that You desire to have a relationship with me. I receive today the free gift of Your grace that You have made available to me. I choose to follow the Lord."

Until Jesus is a part of your life, you will always fear the unknown. Once you are born anew in your spirit and have a relationship with Jesus Christ, you must also recognize that the Holy Spirit lives in you. And you must ask the Holy Spirit to lead, guide, and empower you daily to live the life that the Lord is asking you to live. I encourage you to pray daily, "Father, I receive the gift of Your Holy Spirit to help me today to say and do what is pleasing to You, and to do so with a right spirit, in right timing, and according to right methods. Lead and guide my every step today."

Everyone has moments of anxiety and fear in his life. But a pervasive feeling of anxiousness and fearfulness is *not* God's desire for anyone. Put your faith in what God has done for you by sending Jesus to this earth on your behalf. Place your trust in the Holy Spirit to lead you along life's path with confidence and hope.

> Trust in the LORD with all your heart, And lean not on your own understanding; In all your ways acknowledge Him, And He shall direct your paths.
>
> —Proverbs 3:5-6

What does it mean to "lean on your own understanding"? Give practical examples.

27

↜ What does it mean to "acknowledge" God "in all your ways"? How can these principles help you with anxiety this week?

What Happens if We don't Trust God?

If we choose not to trust God fully with our lives, then we are forced to trust either ourselves or other people. No person can fully care for himself, and no other person or institution can be relied on to provide all that anyone needs. Only God, who has all resources available for His use, can put together a "total provision package" for each person on earth.

If we choose not to trust God with our lives, the results often include:

↜ Increased irritability and frustration with life

↜ Vacillating opinions and little decision making

↜ Repeated errors of judgment

↜ Feelings of persecution

↜ Procrastination

๏ Use of alcohol, drugs, or prescription medications to escape pain, sleeplessness, or nervous tension

๏ Low productivity

๏ A general feeling of restlessness or uneasiness

Jesus referred to such consequences in Matthew 13:3–4, 7, 22:

> Behold, a sower went out to sow. And as he sowed, some seed ... fell among thorns, and the thorns sprang up and choked them ... Now he who received seed among the thorns is he who hears the word, and the cares of this world and the deceitfulness of riches choke the word, and he becomes unfruitful.

Jesus refers to our anxieties as "the cares of this world." They choke the Word of God. A person who becomes self-absorbed with circumstances and self-pursuits is not fully capable of taking in the Word of God. He allows the mundane responsibilities of life to overwhelm him to the point that he gives no thought to God's promises, much less relying upon them in his life.

๏ When have fears and anxieties choked out God's Word in your life?

∾ Which generally causes you more anxiety: "the cares of this world," or "the deceitfulness of riches"? How do these fears choke out God's Word?

∾ Reversing the Trend ∾

How can we reverse this trend? The Scriptures say that we must "take captive" every thought that is contrary to the Word of God. We must recognize our self-absorbed thoughts, capture them, and literally force them into submission, saying to ourselves, "I will not think about this. Rather, I will think about what God says in His Word. I will focus completely on the truth of God, not the facts and opinions that others are feeding me about my situation."

What people tell us always has an element of error in it because it is rooted in humanity or tainted by human frailty; and it is also temporary because no person can see the entire future or past of our lives. What we read in God's Word, however, is true and eternal.

Paul told the Corinthians to use their weapons of spiritual warfare for "casting down arguments and every high thing that exalts itself against the knowledge of God, bringing every thought into captivity to the obedience of Christ" (2 Corinthians 10:5). How do we do this practically?

When times of anxiety and fear seem to overwhelm you, you must make a conscious, deliberate effort to take control over your own thoughts and to bring them into conformity with God's Word.

∾ Five Practical Steps ∾

1. *Read the Gospels.* Calm your own spirit by reading aloud the words of Jesus and the stories about Jesus in the Gospels. Focus especially on what Jesus taught and said. (You may find it beneficial to use a Bible with the words of Jesus highlighted in red.) Don't allow yourself to become distracted or to give up in your reading of God's Word until you feel panic subside and a calmness take root in your heart.

2. *Read the promises of God.* Begin to look up and read aloud the promises of God's Word that pertain to your situation. If you don't know those promises, use a concordance to find them. (Look up a word that relates to your problem, or look up those passages under the heading "fear not.")

3. *Memorize God's promises.* Memorize several of God's promises that seem appropriate for your situation. Read the Bible daily to discover other appropriate passages and memorize them also. Any time that fear attempts to rise up again, recite these promises from God's Word—repeatedly, if need be—until the fear subsides.

4. *Ask the Holy Spirit to take control.* Ask the Holy Spirit to make His promises real in your life. Ask Him to take control of your life and to take control over the situations that are causing you to fear.

5. *Praise God.* Praise God for His goodness and tender loving care in the past. Recall instances in which God has shown Himself to be faithful. Recall instances in which your needs were met, your heart was blessed, and you knew that God was in control of your life. Praise God for His provision and presence in the past.

And then, continue to praise God for who He is—that He is always faithful, which means that what He has done in the past, He will do in the present and the future. Praise God for His goodness—that He can and does work all things together for your eternal good. Praise God for His love that is infinitely deeper and more wonderful than you can fathom.

This discipline puts a stop to anxiety in your life. It reverses the spiraling trend that can so quickly plunge a person into panic or confusion. It pulls your mind and heart back into a proper focus on Jesus Christ and what He did for you on the cross; on the Holy Spirit and what He does for you daily; and on God's power to take care of you now and forever. It gives you a basis in which to root your hope and faith. And it invites the Holy Spirit to deal in a more potent way in and through you, right in the midst of your anxiety.

Follow this five-step process as often as anxiety or fear takes hold of you. You may need to devote a period of time each day to this discipline of reading, reciting, praying, and praising—even several periods of time each day—in order to defeat a pervasive feeling of anxiety or fear. Most of us did not become anxious in a moment, and most of us will not cease to feel anxious instantaneously.

I rise before the dawning of the morning, And cry for help; I hope in Your word. My eyes are awake through the night watches, That I may meditate on Your word.

—Psalm 119:147-148

෨ According to the Psalmist, how might fear and anxiety actually be a blessing?

෨ What does the Psalmist recommend for dealing with fear?

∞ Do Not Be Discouraged ∞

Finally, do not become discouraged if your ability to trust God seems to wax and wane. That is only human. Our ability to trust in God is never absolute—rather, we are to *grow* in our ability to trust God. The decision that we must make is to seek to trust God more. In times of weakness, we need to begin to trust Him. When our trust level is low, we need to trust Him more. Even in times of great trust, we must seek to trust Him *even more*. The wonderful hope that we have, of course, is that the more we trust God, the more we find God to be faithful. Thus, the more we are willing to trust, the more God shows us that we can trust Him.

God's nature has not changed. He is always trustworthy. The more we cast our cares upon Him, the more He shows us how much He truly desires to care for us, give to us, and deliver us from all harm.

And my God shall supply all your need according to His riches
in glory by Christ Jesus.

—Philippians 4:19

❧ What is the difference between "supplying all your need" and
"supplying all your desires"? What insight does this provide into
your own anxieties?

❧ What are Jesus' "riches in glory"? What does this have to do
with your daily needs?

I will instruct you and teach you in the way you should go; I will guide you with My eye.

—Psalm 32:8

Why does God promise to guide you with His eye? How can this calm your fears?

Why does God promise to "instruct you" *and* "to teach you"? What should your response be when you feel confused about the future?

Today and Tomorrow:

Today: The more I study God's Word, the deeper my trust will grow.

Tomorrow: I will spend time this week studying and memorizing God's promises.

35

Strength in Times of Abuse

┌─────────────── ❧ **In This Lesson:** ❧ ───────────────┐

LEARNING: WHAT AM I TO DO ABOUT THE ABUSES THAT I'VE SUFFERED?

GROWING: HOW WILL I FIND GOD'S HEALING FOR THE PAST, PRESENT, AND FUTURE?

└──────────────────────── ✇ ────────────────────────┘

When I was nine years old, my mother married my stepfather, a man who was full of hostility, anger, and bitterness. Never once did I hear this man say that he cared for me or loved me. I don't recall his ever giving me anything. What I do recall are the times when he blew up in anger. He was so abusive that many nights as a teenager I went to bed with a rifle loaded beside me and the door locked. Countless adults today can relate to my experiences. It seems that, in the last two decades, the willingness of our society to confront abuse has greatly increased.

The definition of abuse, however, tends to vary from one person to the next. The extent of *perceived* abuse can also vary from one period in life to the next. Verbal and emotional abuse are more difficult to define than physical or sexual abuse. What is important for our discussion here is that we recognize a fundamental difference between discipline and abuse.

Discipline is given in direct response to a person's actions. It is administered for the ultimate benefit of the person being disciplined; the goal of discipline is altered behavior and a change in the way that a person responds to life. Discipline is an act of love; it is rooted in a desire for a person to be the best that he can be.

Abuse, in sharp contrast, is frequently unrelated to a person's behavior. Totally innocent actions may trigger a violent response in an abuser. Abuse seeks to do a person harm, to inflict pain. It is not corrective. And most important, abuse is manipulative and based on power. At the core of abusive behavior is a desire to control someone else.

We can be certain about two things:

I. It is never God's desire that His children be regularly injured, emotionally or physically. Intense verbal criticism, beatings, and instances of severe deprivation are *not* God's plan for any person.

2. It is never God's desire that His children be sexually abused. Incest, adultery, and fornication are all explicitly forbidden in the Scriptures.

God is never to blame in abusive situations. The blame rests solely with the abuser, and if any underlying spiritual motivation is at work, it comes from the devil, not God. Jesus said clearly, "The thief [the devil] does not come except to steal, and to kill, and to destroy. I have come that they may have life, and that they may have it more abundantly" (John 10:10). God never motivates a person toward abusive behavior.

Responses to Abusive Behavior

The Bible gives us at least six specific things that we can do in abusive situations. All of them allow the Lord to heal us from any damage that has been done to us emotionally, and to free us so that we are able to move forward in our lives without carrying the heavy baggage that results from abuse.

1. Seek God's Guidance

Ask the Lord, "What would You have me do?" No one answer fits all situations. In some cases, God may tell you to move away physically from your abuser. In some cases, the Lord may direct you to receive wise counseling from a Bible-honoring, objective counselor. In still other cases, God may ask you to stay in a relationship with an abusive person and to pray for that person, praying for a transformation in the abuser and your relationship. You will need to ask the Lord for His plan for *you*.

Go to the Lord in prayer, believing that He will direct your path and give you the courage to follow the plan that He reveals to you.

If any of you lacks wisdom, let him ask of God, who gives to all liberally and without reproach, and it will be given to him. But let him ask in faith, with no doubting, for he who doubts is like a wave of the sea driven and tossed by the wind.

—James 1:5-6

๑ What does it mean that God gives "liberally and without reproach"? How does that compare with the way that some humans give?

๑ Describe a wave that is "driven and tossed by the wind." Explain, in your own words, how that picture is similar to a person who asks for wisdom but doubts that it will be given.

2. Pray for Your Abuser

The person who abuses you is a persecutor—not only of you, but of Christ who dwells within you. As you pray for an abuser, ask the Lord to give you insights into the cause of the abusive behavior; these causes can help you as you intercede in prayer for the person. I learned later in my life that my stepfather had a deep anger against his own father because he had been denied an opportunity to pursue the career that he wanted as a young man. Knowing this did not change my stepfather, nor did it lessen my abhorrence for the abuse that I experienced. It did, however, give me a greater compassion to pray for my stepfather.

Pray specifically that your abuser will come into a relationship with the Lord Jesus and that the Lord will deal with his heart. Also pray for boldness to confront your abuser with the message, "That's enough." Abusers expect their victims to run away and hide, cry, shrink back, or fall silent. One of the most beneficial things that you can do is to stand up to your abuser and say, "I am a child of God. I will no longer take your abuse. I'm trusting God to defend me. I'm turning you over to Him, and I'm trusting that He will deal with you."

> "You have heard that it was said, 'YOU SHALL LOVE YOUR NEIGH-BOR and hate your enemy.' But I say to you, love your enemies, bless those who curse you, do good to those who hate you, and pray for those who spitefully use you and persecute you, that you may be sons of your Father in heaven; for He makes His sun rise on the evil and on the good, and sends rain on the just and on the unjust."
>
> —Matthew 5:43-45

✍ Why does Jesus tell us that God "makes His sun rise on the evil and on the good"? What does this suggest about why we are commanded to love our enemies?

✍ In what ways does loving your enemies make you a "son of your Father in heaven"?

3. Forgive Your Abuser

Choose to forgive the person who has abused you, and also any person who contributed or "stood by" as you were abused. Forgiveness does not mean that the abuse didn't happen, nor does it mean that the abuse was not an important issue in your life. What it means is that you are "letting go" of any anger, hurt, bitterness, or pain associated with the abuse. You are trusting God to deal with your abuser. Forgiveness is an act of releasing the person—not to "go free" without any consequences for his behavior, but releasing the person into the hands of the Lord and *His* consequences.

Part of forgiveness is not taking revenge into your own hands. Refuse to retaliate against your abuser. Leave all acts of vengeance to God.

> "For if you forgive men their trespasses, your heavenly Father will also forgive you. But if you do not forgive men their trespasses, neither will your Father forgive your trespasses."

> —Matthew 6:14-15

∾ Why is it important to forgive others who have wronged you?

∾ How often does God forgive *your* sins? How often might you have to choose to forgive others?

41

4. Open Yourself to God's Healing

Many people who have been abused continue to suffer from nightmares or memories for years after the abuse occurred. If you are experiencing these abused emotions, it is vitally important that you develop a habit of filling your mind with God's Word, especially just before you go to bed at night. Listen to messages—either spoken or in song—that fill your mind with God's Word and statements of God's love, goodness, and grace toward you. You may want to listen to Bible tapes or read aloud from God's Word. If memories of abuse haunt you, address them in the name of Jesus, saying, "Lord, I'm trusting You to turn my thoughts toward what is good, right, and beneficial for me." Speak to your dreams or memories: "You are not of God, and you no longer have a place in my mind. I give you to Christ Jesus, and I choose to think of what He has done for me rather than what has been done to me by others."

Ask the Lord to replace your bad memories of abuse with positive images of the ways in which the Lord has extended His love to you.

> Finally, brethren, whatever things are true, whatever things are noble, whatever things are just, whatever things are pure, whatever things are lovely, whatever things are of good report, if there is any virtue and if there is anything praiseworthy— meditate on these things.
>
> —Philippians 4:8

Explain in your own words what things are: true; noble; just; pure; lovely; of good report.

🙞 Make a list below of some things that you can meditate on when unwelcome thoughts or memories flood your mind.

5. Choose to Pursue the Truth About Yourself

Those who are abused nearly always come to believe lies about themselves at some point. They believe that they deserve the abuse, that they are unworthy of love, or that they are inept or incapable of succeeding in life. These are all lies, and they need to be labeled as such!

The truth needs to be proclaimed aloud by the victim of abuse: "The truth is that I can do all things through Christ Jesus. I am a joint heir in Christ Jesus of all God's benefits. I am in line to receive God's rewards. Christ in me has the power, strength, and ability, and together we will succeed in this."

Each of us has room for growth and improvement, but the abuser rarely focuses on specific areas of fault or error. Rather, an abuser gives generalized "labels" to his victims, using such phrases as, "You always," "You never," or "You will never." Labels such as these are a sure indicator that a lie is being told because the truth of God is that we *can* become more than we are today, we *can* be forgiven, and that God holds out hope for us that tomorrow can be brighter than today. Every time a negative self-criticism comes to mind, the abused person needs to respond, "That's a lie! I will not believe that. It isn't true according to God's Word."

These ... things the LORD hates ... A false witness who speaks lies, And one who sows discord among brethren.

—Proverbs 6:16. 19

෴ How is it a lie when someone tells you that you are worthless or a failure? Give Bible passages that support your answer.

෴ How does God respond when we tell someone that he is a failure or worthless? How do such lies "sow discord among brethren"?

6. Move Forward Positively in Your Life

Believe that God will bring something good out of your past experience. Never let an abuser dictate the course of your life or keep you from doing what you know the Lord is leading you to do. Part of moving forward in your life is believing that the cycle of abuse in your life has been broken—and is being broken—by your change of behavior.

44

We are called to say, "That may be the way I was or the situation that I was in, but I am redeemed by Christ Jesus. I am in the process of being transformed into His image. I am in the process of being healed."

Trust God to bring something good out of an abusive situation. The Lord truly can create something wonderful in you and through you, no matter how you may have been hurt by others in the past. He can make you strong where you are weak, whole in areas where you feel shattered, and healthy in areas where you have been injured.

> And we know that all things work together for good to those who love God, to those who are the called according to His purpose.
>
> —Romans 8:28

✎ Why does Paul say that "all things work together for good"? Why not, "all things are good"?

✎ What things are needed from God for all things to "work together for good"? What is needed from you?

45

Speaking God's Love to Yourself

If you are a victim of abuse, let me assure you that you are loved by God, you are loved by your fellow Christians, and you are worthy to be loved—not because of what you have done or what has been done to you, but because of who you are: a child of God, fully adopted into His family, and fully deserving of the love of your fellow brothers and sisters in Christ Jesus.

If nobody else is around to speak the Lord's love into your life, I encourage you to speak God's love to yourself today. Say aloud, "I am God's child. He loves me—yes, me!" Let the truth of those words sink deep into your soul. Let them heal the hurt that you have known and the shame that you have felt. Let God's love for you wipe away your tears and restore you to wholeness.

> If your enemy is hungry, give him bread to eat; And if he is thirsty, give him water to drink; For so you will heap coals of fire on his head, And the LORD will reward you.
>
> —Proverbs 25:21-22

∾ What does it mean to "heap coals of fire" on another person's head. How does helping a person in need accomplish this?

✎ Why does the Lord reward us when we "heap coals of fire" on someone's head?

Do not be overcome by evil, but overcome evil with good.

—Romans 12:21

✎ When have you been "overcome by evil"? In practical terms, how might you have "overcome evil with good" in that situation?

✎ Today and Tomorrow: ✐

TODAY: BEING HEALED OF ABUSE INVOLVES SEEING MYSELF AS GOD SEES ME.

TOMORROW: I WILL DELIBERATELY CHOOSE TO FORGIVE THOSE WHO HAVE ABUSED ME RIGHT NOW—AND AGAIN AS NEEDED IN THE FUTURE.

Strength in Times of Criticism

❧ In This Lesson: ❧

LEARNING: AM I REALLY A FAILURE IF THAT'S WHAT I'VE ALWAYS BEEN
TOLD?

GROWING: HOW CAN I FIND OUT WHAT IS *REALLY* TRUE ABOUT ME?

Each of us experiences criticism from time to time. In some cases, it is a part of discipline to teach us how to improve in a particular skill, attitude, or behavior. Pervasive criticism, however, can have a wounding and weakening effect.

Through much of my childhood, I received numerous messages that reinforced the idea that I wasn't good for anything, wasn't worth anything, and would never amount to anything. I tried very hard to please, but several factors seemed to work against me in those days. One of the factors was that I had started school a year before my peers, so I was always the youngest person in my class; therefore, I also tended to be the smallest and skinniest. Another factor was that my mother made me wear short pants until I went to junior high school, and then I wore knickers and long socks. Nobody else wore knickers! Yet another factor was that I grew up in a poor environment. Several of our apartments were in the basements of buildings. From my perspective as a child, everybody was "higher" than we were.

To counterbalance these negative messages, I also had some positive influences—in particular a schoolteacher named Mrs. Ferrell and a Sunday school teacher named Craig Stowe. These two people gave me important signs of approval when I needed them desperately. They were like beacons in a wilderness of disapproval.

Many people carry emotional baggage associated with intense or pervasive criticism. They express it by saying, "Nobody cared," "I never heard a word of praise when I was growing up," or "Nobody ever said to me, 'Good job.'" They express the criticism that they heard as children in a wide variety of self-demeaning actions or in self-deprecating statements.

Perhaps the foremost thing that we need to recognize is that criticism *damages* a person on the inside. It wounds a person in his emotions.

&. When have you been the recipient of on-going, intense criticism?

&. What happens to a person who is severely criticized over a prolonged period of time?

Get the Right Opinion

Criticism is nearly always registered at what a person isn't doing right or a person's lack of desirable qualities. A perceived lack of goodness brings about a perceived state of badness. It is no wonder that those who are criticized over a long period come to the conclusion, "I'm worthless. I'm no good. I can't make it. I'll never do any better." They have been fed a message of what they *aren't* so often that they have lost all sight of what they *are*.

The first step toward overcoming the emotional wounds of criticism is to get the right perspective on one's true worth. If we continue to hold a feeling of inadequacy and low value, we are denying what God Himself says about us. On the other hand, when we set our eyes on who God says we are and what God thinks about us, we begin to gain a biblical perspective on our value.

God bases our worth not on *what* we have, but on *whom* we have— Jesus Christ as our personal Savior, and the Holy Spirit as our ever-present Comforter and Counselor. If you have accepted Jesus Christ as your Savior, you have *all that it takes* to have everlasting value in God's eyes! God bases our worth, not on our performance or achievements, but on whether we have received His free gift of grace and forgiveness in our lives. God bases our worth not on where we live or how we look, but on whether we know, follow, and trust Jesus Christ as our Lord.

As long as a person bases his value on personal achievements, associations, or wealth, value will remain low. When a person bases his worth on his relationship with God, value soars. When we look at what we have done and can do by ourselves, we inevitably come to the conclusion that we are lacking in ability. When we look, however, at all that God wants us to do, equips us to do, and promises to enable us to do, we lack no ability. When it comes to who you are and what you are destined to do in life, there's only one opinion that truly matters—the Lord's opinion!

> Therefore, if anyone is in Christ, he is a new creation; old things have passed away; behold, all things have become new.
>
> —2 Corinthians 5:17

᷋ Have you accepted Christ as your Savior? If so, you are a new creation. If not, what is preventing you from doing so right now?

᷋ If you are a new creation in Christ, what does that say about any criticism that you have received in the past? What does it say about criticism from people in the future?

᷒ What Is the Lord's Opinion of You? ᷒

The Lord says that you are His workmanship. This means that you are of notable excellence solely because He made you. You are a prized example of His creation. God looked at all that He made in Genesis and declared, "It is good." That's the way that the Lord looks upon you as His creation. He doesn't make inferior or worthless human beings. The Lord is a master Craftsman who produces only valuable people.

The Lord says that He removed your sin nature the moment that you be-lieved in Christ Jesus as your Savior. The only thing about your creation that can keep you from the presence of God is the sin nature with which you were born. Once you have received Christ Jesus as your Savior, that sin nature has been changed. You are "born again" with a new spiritual nature that puts you into a completely reconciled relationship with God. The one negative aspect of your being has been removed forever! You are valuable to the Lord as His creation, and you are also forgiven and gain full status as one whom the Lord can use and bless fully for His purposes.

The Lord says that He has created and saved you for a future of good works. The Lord has already designed what those good works are to be. God had a purpose in mind for you even before you were born. He has a role for you to fill and a place for you to live as His child on this earth. Furthermore, with the Holy Spirit living in you, the Lord declares that you are equipped, empowered, and enabled to succeed in all that He calls you to do.

> I have been crucified with Christ; it is no longer I who live, but Christ lives in me; and the life which I now live in the flesh I live by faith in the Son of God, who loved me and gave Himself for me.
>
> —Galatians 2:20

Why did Jesus love *you* enough to die for you? What bearing does this have on the criticisms of other people?

∞ What does Paul mean when he says, "it is no longer I who live, but Christ lives in me"? If Christ lives in you, then who is being persecuted when you are *unfairly* criticized?

∞ Refuse to Perpetuate a Cycle of Criticism ∞

The person who is hurt by abuse has a built-in tendency to hurt others in the same area. Those who are criticized harshly for a long period tend to be more critical of others or to continue the pattern of criticism by downgrading themselves.

Ask the Lord to help you put a stop to both patterns. Refuse to ridicule others. Instead, choose to praise and encourage others, building up their strengths. Focus on their assets and positive attributes, rather than their deficits and flaws. The person who praises the good work of the Lord in others is an "edifier"—one who builds up others and encourages them in their faith walk. We are called repeatedly in the Scriptures to be edifiers.

Refuse to downgrade yourself in the presence of others or to engage in behaviors that send a message that you do not care about your appearance, your reputation, or your responsibilities.

> Let all bitterness, wrath, anger, clamor, and evil speaking be put away from you, with all malice. And be kind to one another, tenderhearted, forgiving one another, even as God in Christ forgave you.
>
> —Ephesians 4:31-32

❧ Give practical examples of these negative behaviors: wrath; anger; clamor; evil speaking; malice.

❧ Give practical examples of the *opposite* of the above behaviors.

∽ Get the Right Perspective on Perfection ∽

Those who experience years of criticism often strive for perfection in an effort to prove themselves worthy or valuable to others. The perfectionist is usually a person who is less likely to appraise abilities and attributes realistically. Feeling that he is worth nothing and incapable of anything but failure, the perfectionist then seeks to succeed at all costs.

The truth is that nobody can live up to God's perfection. Nobody can "get it right" all the time. Nobody can live a totally sin-free life. Nobody can escape all temptation. Romans 3:23 clearly states, "All have sinned and fall short of the glory of God."

You may ask, "But what about those verses in the Bible that call us to be perfect?" When the Bible speaks of perfection, it is referring to what we call "wholeness." To be perfect, a person would have to be whole, and to be made whole is to be made perfect. God calls us to pursue wholeness at all times. But the Lord also tells us plainly in His Word that He is the One who makes us whole; we cannot make ourselves whole. The way to "perfection," therefore, is to trust God to do His perfecting work in us. We are not to struggle to become perfect or knock ourselves out trying to get everything right all the time. He'll do the work in us and bring about His perfection in His timing, using His methods, and all for His purposes.

In 1 John 2:1 we read, "My little children, these things I write to you, that you may not sin." But then the verse continues, "And if anyone sins, we have an Advocate with the Father, Jesus Christ the righteous." It's as if God is saying to us, "Little children, I don't want you to sin. I've given you My Word so that you can grow up and avoid sinning. But if and when you sin, I've made provision for that, too." Recognize that you aren't who you once were, and that the Lord is continuing to mold and make you. Trust Him to be your potter (see Jeremiah 18:1–6).

And He said to me, "My grace is sufficient for you, for My strength is made perfect in weakness." Therefore most gladly I will rather boast in my infirmities, that the power of Christ may rest upon me.

—2 Corinthians 12:9

When have you seen the strength of God "made perfect" in your own life through your weakness?

ⸯ How can you use this verse as an answer to those who criticize you unfairly? How can you use it to stop striving for perfection?

∞ Have the Right Desire to Please ∞

Those who have suffered from criticism often have a great desire to please others. They go above and beyond the call of duty in trying to serve, thereby gaining the approval of those in authority over them. As Christians, we are always called to do our best with the talents and gifts that God has given us. We are not, however, called to:

ⸯ compare ourselves to others, hoping that "in comparison," we will look better, or

ⸯ seek the approval of others if that approval is contrary to God's commandments.

God doesn't grade on the curve. He always judges our behavior against the absolute standard of His commandments. Furthermore, God is not merciful to us on the basis of whether other people like us, but solely on the basis of our acceptance of Jesus Christ. We gain nothing by comparing ourselves to others or seeking to win popularity among our peers. A desire to please God is manifested in three main ways:

I. A desire to allow the Holy Spirit to transform us.

2. A willingness to trust God to lead us where He chooses, and to use us in ways that He designs.

3. A commitment to doing what the Lord calls us to do, even if it is contrary to the values of the world.

To truly please God, we must be willing to change and to grow ever more into the likeness of Jesus Christ. We must be willing to go wherever the Lord leads us and do whatever He puts commands. The Lord doesn't ask us to succeed in the eyes of others, but He does ask us to live a life that is acceptable to Him. Jesus never said, "Do your best." He said, "Follow Me." If we truly desire to please the Lord, we *will* follow Him and become His disciples.

> And do not be conformed to this world, but be transformed by the renewing of your mind, that you may prove what is that good and acceptable and perfect will of God.

> —Romans 12:2

§ What does it mean to be "conformed to this world"? Give practical examples from your own life.

§ How does one "renew" his mind? How does renewing your mind help you to discover the "perfect will of God"?

For you were once darkness, but now you are light in the Lord. Walk as children of light (for the fruit of the Spirit is in all goodness, righteousness, and truth), finding out what is acceptable to the Lord.

—Ephesians 5:8-10

๛ What, in practical terms, does it mean to "walk as children of light"? How does this walk help you to be "finding out what is acceptable to the Lord"?

๛ If you are walking in the light of Christ, what value can other people's criticism have? How can you know when to take criticism to heart and when to reject it as a lie?

๛ Today and Tomorrow: ๛

TODAY: GOD'S PERSPECTIVE OF ME IS THE ONLY ONE THAT MATTERS, AND I MUST THINK OF MYSELF AS HE THINKS OF ME.

TOMORROW: I WILL STUDY GOD'S WORD THIS WEEK, DELIBERATELY STRIVING TO RENEW MY MIND.

Lesson 6

Strength in Times of Guilt

┌─────────────── ❧ **In This Lesson:** ☙ ───────────────┐

Learning: What is the meaning of my constant guilt feelings?

Growing: How can I find lasting freedom from sin *and* guilt?

─────────────────── ∞ ───────────────────
└──┘

Most people develop their concept of God upon the behavior of their parents. My father died when I was nine months old, and when he died, a little bit of my concept about God was established that said, in effect, "God has left you, too." My mother worked full-time, and I spent many hours alone after school. I came to believe, "God is away somewhere with somebody else." God was remote to me, and He was a hard, harsh God from my perspective as a lonely, anxious child. He was authority—and in that regard, He was very much like my stepfather: mean, abusive, out to put me down.

I had seen God's hand at work in my church and in my grandfather's life to the point that I had the faith to believe in Him. I knew the Bible stories well enough to know about Jesus and what He had done in giving His life on the cross. Still, God was such a mystery that I never felt that He was accessible to me. I had a strong feeling that I needed to be more holy so that God might come closer. No matter how much I read the Bible, I felt that I could have read it more. No matter how much I prayed, I felt that I could have prayed more. I felt certain that God was keeping score on every aspect of my behavior, and the end result was the heavy emotional baggage of pervasive guilt.

Through the years, many people have told me that they have had a similar experience in their lives. They have spent years trying to

- ✎ get good enough for God to approve of them

- ✎ perform for God so that He might reward them

- ✎ do enough good works to earn God's favor

The good news of the gospel, however, is this: we are not saved according to our works, but according to the grace of God. We can never earn our salvation. It is a free gift from God. As Paul clearly taught the Romans, "If you confess with your mouth the Lord Jesus and believe in your heart that God has raised Him from the dead, you will be saved. For with the heart one believes unto righteousness, and with the mouth confession is made unto salvation" (Romans 10:9–10). The provision for your salvation has been made in full by Jesus Christ. There's nothing more that you can add to it. You can only receive this free gift of God's mercy and love.

The first step toward removing the emotional pain of guilt in your life is to receive God's forgiveness. This means accepting Jesus Christ as your personal Savior and inviting God to cleanse your heart and create in you a new spiritual nature. Have you come to that point in your life? If not, I invite you to pray today:

> "Lord, I accept what Jesus Christ did on the cross for my sake. I receive Him as my Savior today. I accept Your offer of forgiveness. I believe that You are completely cleansing me of my old sin nature and that You are creating in me a new spiritual nature. I receive the presence of the Holy Spirit into my life, and I ask You to help me live in conformity to Jesus Christ. It is in Jesus' name that I pray. Amen."

ซ. If you prayed that prayer, sign your name below with today's date. Keep this book as a record of this momentous day. If you accepted Christ in the past, write that date below.

What Happens When Christians Sin?

I would like to tell you that, after I received Jesus Christ at the age of 12, all feelings of guilt were completely removed from my life. That is not so, however. The emotional baggage of pervasive guilt continued to manifest itself periodically.

This does not mean that my salvation was invalid. I have absolutely no doubt that my conversion was genuine, that my spiritual nature was changed, and that my heart was cleansed and forgiven on that day. What I had to face, however, was what all Christians have to face—that we continue to sin, to break God's commandments, and to give in to temptation, even after we are born again. In my years of experience as a pastor, I have concluded that most Christians don't know what to do when they continue to sin after salvation. Let's take a look at what the Bible has to say about this.

First, the Bible says that, after we have experienced God's free gift of grace, our *desire* for sin diminishes. Paul asked, "Shall we continue in sin that grace may abound?" He answered his own question, "Certainly not!" (Romans 6:1–2). The desire for sin is greatly diminished upon experiencing God's forgiveness.

Second, the Bible acknowledges that we sin, even after we are born again. Paul also admitted to the Romans, "I do what I don't want to do, and I don't do what I want to do" (Romans 7:15). It is in those times

61

that we must say to God, "I'm struggling. I'm not doing well. I'm failing. Please forgive me and help me." Forgiveness is granted to the Christian the moment it is requested. Our *feeling* forgiven, however, may take some time.

Third, the Bible says that we grow in our understanding of God's grace (see 2 Peter 3:18). The more we become like Jesus Christ and are conformed to His will and likeness, the more we realize the awesome nature of God and how great the gulf is between God and mankind. Our salvation becomes an ever-increasing miracle to us. We have an increasing desire to guard our hearts against the temptations of the devil because our salvation is so precious to us.

Fourth, the Bible teaches that, every time we have an awareness of our sin, we are to ask for God's forgiveness. There never is a time when we should feel that we are "beyond" God's ability to forgive us. I have met Christians who say, "Well, I've sinned so many times since I was saved, I'm not sure if God will forgive me one more time," or "I've committed a sin even though I *knew* better. How can God forgive that?"

The fact is, God forgives *all* our sin. We cannot fathom such mercy, but it is real, nonetheless. Surely if Jesus taught His disciples that they were to forgive other people up to "seventy times seven" for sins committed against them, our heavenly Father is able to forgive us that many times and more!

> If we confess our sins, He is faithful and just to forgive us our sins and to cleanse us from all unrighteousness.
>
> —1 John 1:9

⚘ What sins does this verse cover? Are there sins that this verse does *not* apply to?

⚘ What is the difference between "forgive us our sins" and "cleanse us from all unrighteousness"? Why does God do both?

Letting Go of Your Past

Once you have requested God's forgiveness, the next vital step toward being free from guilt is to let go of your past.

In the course of my ministry, I have met countless people who are haunted by their sins. They have not been able to forgive themselves and let go of their past. The Bible tells us that, once we have repented of our sins, God both forgives them and forgets them (see Isaiah 43:25). It is not the Lord, therefore, who reminds you of past sins that you have already confessed to Him. Rather, it is the one whom the Bible calls the "accuser of our brethren," the devil (Revelation 12:10). When you are confronted with images or memories of sins that you have already confessed to God, it's time to say, "I refuse to accept these thoughts. God has already forgiven me of that. I'm letting this go."

"I, even I, am He who blots out your transgressions for My own sake; And I will not remember your sins."

—Isaiah 43:25

⮜ According to this verse, why does God "blot out your transgressions"? What does this tell you about His willingness to forgive?

⮜ What kind of record does God keep of your past sins? What kind of record do **you** keep?

∽ Mistakes ∽

We must always remember that sins and mistakes are different from each other. A sin is a choice to do something that we know is against God's will. It is a willful act—one that is calculated, thought out, anticipated, and fully conscious. It is deliberately flying in the face of what we know is right in God's eyes.

A mistake, on the other hand, is usually spur of the moment, unplanned, and made without forethought. A mistake is a miscalculation, an error in judgment. We are to own up to our mistakes and learn from them. We are to make amends if we have hurt anyone in our mistakes. We are to ask God to help us not to make the same mistake again.

We must *not,* however, beat ourselves up emotionally over the mistakes that we make. To err is human. As long as we are alive, we are going to make mistakes.

∞ False Guilt ∞

False guilt occurs when a person feels the guilt that appropriately belongs to another person. This kind of guilt is often experienced by those who are the victims of abuse or rejection. Parents whose adult children rebel against God's Word also tend to feel this guilt. These people feel that they must have failed in some way and that they have contributed to the rise of the abusive behavior, rejection, or rebellion. Therefore, they feel guilty for having caused the sin of someone else. If you are holding on to false guilt, you must let go of it. Ask the Lord to free you from all guilt that is associated with sins that aren't your own.

∞ When have you struggled with guilt over mistakes?

∞ When have you struggled with false guilt? How has the Lord dealt with you in these cases?

Guilt for Having "Missed God"

Some people feel that they have missed something that God wanted them to do—that the Lord called them to do something for Him and they failed to do it. They feel guilty as a result. I encourage these people to ask themselves two questions. 1) "Was that call really of God, or was it something of my own desire?" If the call was not truly from God, God does not hold a person responsible for fulfilling it. 2) "Did I have a direct opportunity to fulfill that call and turn away from it?" In some cases, people feel a rather vague call of God toward a particular area of service, but an opportunity has never presented itself to become involved in that area of ministry. They should feel no guilt for having failed God.

If, however, you feel that you had a specific call from God and a specific opportunity to fulfill it, but you did not, today is the day to turn to the Lord and say, "Lord, I'm sorry that I disobeyed You. I ask You to forgive me. Whatever You want me to do from this point on, I'll do it." Take courage from the life of Jonah. He had a very specific call, and he turned his back on it. God gave him a second chance, and He'll give you a second chance, too.

> ...Revive us, and we will call upon Your name. Restore us, O LORD God of hosts; Cause Your face to shine, And we shall be saved!

> —Psalm 80:18-19

◈ Are you struggling with a sense of guilt? If so, pray the above prayer in your own words, then write the date below and keep this as a record. You have been forgiven!

Guilt That Arises from a False Concept of God

A pervasive feeling of guilt is a *feeling* that many people have. I, too, have experienced this feeling in the past. This feeling has nothing to do with what a person *knows* to be true about the Scriptures and about what it means to be saved or forgiven. It is a feeling that is rooted in our perception of God.

As I shared earlier, I grew up believing God to be a very harsh, hard judge. I felt that I had to be perfect in order for God to accept me and love me and, since I knew that I wasn't perfect, I had feelings of guilt that I had failed God and that I continued to fail Him daily. What was wrong here was not my sinful state—that had been changed the moment I accepted Jesus as my Savior—but my concept of God. It took years for me to acquire an accurate concept of God and to come to the point where I could feel genuine love flowing between God and me. I'm not talking about just saying, "I love You" to God. I'm talking about deep, intimate feelings of love both for and from God.

If you are struggling with a false perception of God, I encourage you to take a long, hard look at the Gospels. Jesus is a perfect reflection of God the Father. He didn't do anything that was contrary to the nature and desire of His heavenly Father. Jesus was tender with children. He extended forgiveness to sinners whom the rest of society was ready to stone to death. He healed all the sick that were brought to Him. He loved others so much that He was prepared to die for their sins.

Your abusive parent is not the image of God. The teacher, coach, or other authority figure who treated you harshly is not the image of God. Jesus is! It is Jesus who longs to wrap His arms around you and say to you, "Come with Me to visit My Father. He can hardly wait to meet you."

God understands your frailties and weaknesses, and He loves you with a deep, unchanging love in spite of them. God's love for you is unconditional—He does not place any "ifs," "whens," or any other qualifiers on His love. Don't limit God's capacity to love. It is infinite, and it extends to you in all situations and conditions.

Refuse to trust your *feelings* about God. Trust, instead, the truth presented in God's Word. Base how you feel on the sure foundation of God's love as revealed by Jesus. You and only you know if you have a right understanding of God and a right relationship with God. If you are not "right" with God, you can be. The Lord stands ready at all times to forgive you and to receive you fully into His presence. The Lord's desire for you today is that you be free of guilt and sin. All you need to do is to take Him up on His offer to carry the load of your guilt and sin.

> For God so loved the world that He gave His only begotten Son, that whoever believes in Him should not perish but have everlasting life. For God did not send His Son into the world to condemn the world, but that the world through Him might be saved.
>
> —John 3:16-17

⮞ Why did Jesus come into the world, according to this passage? What does that suggest about His willingness to forgive sins?

How do you think God felt when Jesus died on the cross? What does that level of love for *you* suggest about God's grace?

> Then Peter came to Him and said, "Lord, how often shall my brother sin against me, and I forgive him? Up to seven times?" Jesus said to him, "I do not say to you, up to seven times, but up to seventy times seven."
>
> —Matthew 18:21-22

When have you forgiven someone for sins over and over again? Did you keep track of how many times? Did it reach to 490?

How many times has God forgiven *you* for individual sins in your life? Did *that* number reach 490?

As a father pities his children, So the LORD pities those who fear Him. For He knows our frame; He remembers that we are dust.

—Psalm 103:13-14

❧ Why does God "know our frame"? What does it mean that "we are dust"?

❧ How does our "frame" affect our actions? How does this increase God's fatherly pity?

❧ Today and Tomorrow: ❧

Today: When I sin, God is not taken by surprise; yet He is always ready to forgive.

Tomorrow: I will ask the Lord to show me the difference between legitimate guilt and false guilt.

Lesson 7

Strength in Times of Frustration

❧ In This Lesson: ❧

Learning: What is the cause of life's countless frustrations?

Growing: How do I overcome an on-going frustration with life?

There was never a time when I felt God say directly to me, *I want you to preach.* But from the time I was saved, I never really thought about doing anything else. To me, preaching always seemed to be what I was destined to do.

I came to adulthood with a heavy load of emotional baggage—lots of insecurities, a lifelong feeling of loneliness—so being a pastor was probably one of the least likely things that I *should* have aspired to do. Being a pastor meant dealing with lots of people, and I had virtually no experience with that. It also meant being in a leadership position, and again, nothing in my background had prepared me for such a role.

In my feelings of inadequacy, I drove myself to be the most perfect pastor who had ever lived. I studied long and hard, prayed long and hard, and worked long and hard. I drove myself—and I drove other people. I wanted God's approval, but I also wanted the approval of those who called me to be their pastor. I did what most perfectionists would do:

~ I exerted control. I felt that I had to be in control, no matter what was happening.

~ I was combative. No matter what was going on, I was ready to fight if somebody wanted to fight—not physically, of course, but intellectually and spiritually.

~ I was critical. If a person didn't live up to my standard, I let my disapproval be known.

I was wrong on all three counts, and I also became constantly irritated and frustrated. Irritation and frustration are inner events. The person with pervasive feelings of irritation and frustration as a general rule:

*~ hasn't dealt with something

*~ is running from something

*~ hasn't identified something

*~ refuses to confront his own inner anger

Irritation and frustration are often rooted in an inability to accept the way that God has created me, a reluctance to face a problem in the past, or a refusal to confront something that I know is wrong and contrary to God's purposes and plan. I have met countless people who have a deep inner frustration that never seems to leave them. I usually ask them, "Why are you striving so hard? What are you expecting to earn?"

~ Is it a matter of pride—do you desire to be recognized?

~ Is it a matter of control—are you seeking greater power?

Is it a matter of inadequacy—do you believe that you must do more in order to be loved?

If so, I have good news for you. God couldn't possibly love you more than He loves you right now. If you are attempting to earn His approval, you already have it! God's word to you is, "Let Me do the striving on your behalf. Let Me do the work in you. Receive My love and forgiveness. Receive My help. Accept My offer and let Me do My perfecting work in you."

When have you experienced prolonged periods of frustration in your life? What circumstances caused the frustration? What underlying issues in your spirit might have been the root cause?

The LORD has appeared of old to me, saying: "Yes, I have loved you with an everlasting love; Therefore with lovingkindness I have drawn you."

—Jeremiah 31:3

When does "an everlasting love" begin? When does it end? What does this suggest about your ability to earn God's love?

God-Given Frustration

There are times when irritability is not rooted in failure or a desire for perfection. Rather, God seems to place in your spirit a type of restlessness. This type of frustration can be differentiated by four qualities:

1. You are not trying to conquer anybody or anything.

2. The onset of the frustration is usually quite sudden and intense, even though there seems to be no cause for it.

3. The frustration is not with anybody else but with yourself alone.

4. The frustration ends the moment that you move into the new path that God is leading you to walk.

When this type of frustration manifests itself in your life, be glad! God is plowing up your soul and forcing you to confront a deeper part of your character. He is doing a work in you that is for your growth and eternal good. Most people are familiar with Romans 8:28: "We know that all things work together for good to those who love God, to those who are the called according to His purpose." The next two verses go on to tell us God's purpose in working all things for our good: so that we might be transformed into the likeness of Jesus Christ.

For whom He foreknew, He also predestined to be conformed to the image of His Son, that He might be the firstborn among many brethren. Moreover whom He predestined, these He also called; whom He called, these He also justified; and whom He justified, these He also glorified.

—Romans 8:29–30

When you have a churning feeling deep inside you—a restlessness in your soul—consider the possibility that God is "justifying" you to conform with the image of Christ Jesus. Face up to any sins that the Lord may reveal to you during this time. Read God's Word with renewed vigor, be alert to those verses that God may cause to leap off the page as you read them. Start *expecting* God to show you what He is leading you to do. Thank the Lord for getting you ready for His next step in your life!

↝ According to Romans 8:29–30 (above), what is the process of becoming "conformed to the image" of Jesus?

↝ What is involved in each of these steps, on God's part? On your part?

Compulsions and Obsessions

Frustration at times results in compulsions and obsessions. These frequently are related to perfectionism. Compulsions and obsessions are traps, not blessings. They drive a person to pursue something until he gains it, regardless of who may be hurt in the process or what damage may be caused. Frustration can also lead to greed, which is a form of obsession. The more people want, the more there is to want.

❧ Pause for a moment and reflect about the things that you truly value in life. What would you *not* want to lose? What do you most desire to have when you are 90 years old?

Most people will list such things as:

   ❧ a long, fruitful, and fulfilled life

   ❧ good health

   ❧ a loving circle of family and friends

   ❧ the hope of eternal life

   ❧ inner peace and joy

I have good news and bad news regarding these things. The bad news is that you cannot get any of these things on your own. You cannot buy them or earn them. The good news is that these are the very things that the Lord desires for you, and He will help you to experience them as you trust in Him.

How do you feel when you are not in control of situations? What do you do with those feelings?

Set your mind on things above, not on things on the earth. For you died, and your life is hidden with Christ in God.

—Colossians 3:2-3

What does it mean that "your life is hidden with Christ in God"?

If your life is hidden in God, how might you revise your list of priorities on the previous page?

Frustration with Other People

There are times when it is natural to feel frustration on a short-term basis. This frustration is sometimes related to the actions of another person, generally from conflicting preferences, opinions, or personality traits. At times it is related to circumstances that are beyond our control. What are we to do in those times?

The Bible teaches that we can experience a continual feeling of inner contentment *regardless of our outward circumstances.* The apostle Paul was sitting in a Roman prison, facing all kinds of persecution and ridicule from others, when he wrote, "I have learned in whatever state I am, to be content: I know how to be abased, and I know how to abound. Everywhere and in all things I have learned both to be full and to be hungry, both to abound and to suffer need" (Philippians 4:11–12).

How did Paul find inner contentment? By focusing on the sovereignty of God, rather than on the will of people. By praising and thanking God, rather than criticizing others. By putting trust in God to deal with the future, rather than continually looking at the past. By trusting in God to make all things right, rather than distrusting human ability.

Paul turned his attention to Christ and away from his circumstances and detractors, and he received strength. His contentment did not rest in a denial of the outside world or of his situation. His contentment flowed from his trust in Christ Jesus. The answer to frustration comes as you trust God, whether your inner restlessness is related to unresolved issues in your past, to people or situations over which you have no control, or to a God-given restlessness intended to draw you deeper into the Lord's will.

  Recall the most frustrating experience of your life. What did you do? What was the result?

Be anxious for nothing, but in everything by prayer and suppli-cation, with thanksgiving, let your requests be made known to God; and the peace of God, which surpasses all understanding, will guard your hearts and minds through Christ Jesus.

—Philippians 4:6-7

  Why does Paul tell us to make our requests "with thanks-giving"?

∽ List below some of the things that are making you anxious today, then "let your requests be made known to God" in a time of prayer and thanksgiving.

Frustration Rooted in Impatience

Finally, there are times when our feelings of frustration are rooted simply in a hurry-up attitude. We become impatient with the timing of certain events or changes that we desire in our lives.

A restlessness in spirit can lead to a tendency to run past God's will. You may know what God wants you to do, and in eagerness to get the job done, you forget that God also has a perfect timetable for accomplishing His will. Just as the Lord has a right thing for you to do, so He also has a right time for each step that He leads you to take.

The Bible repeatedly shows us the advantages of "waiting on the Lord." Waiting means saying to the Lord, "Is now the time? I'm waiting until You give me the green light before I go." If you have a pattern of getting ahead of God's timing, ask yourself, "Why do I keep running right past God's will in trying to get it? What am I in a hurry for?"

The disadvantages of getting ahead of God are evident throughout the Bible. Abraham and Sarah got ahead of God's plan when Abraham fathered a child through Hagar. Peter was notorious for trying to get ahead of God's plan, even slicing off a man's ear in the Garden of Gethsemane. Jesus, on the other hand, never showed up too early or too late. He always arrived right on time, in keeping with what the Father was doing. Learning to wait on God's timing is one of the hallmarks of the mature Christian life.

> Wait on the LORD; Be of good courage, And He shall strengthen your heart; Wait, I say, on the LORD!
>
> —Psalm 27:14

When have you rushed ahead of God's timing? What was the long-term result?

Why does the Psalmist tell us to "be of good courage" when waiting on the Lord? Why is courage needed? Where do we find that courage?

The Lord doesn't catapult us into greatness; He grows us into spiritual maturity. He stretches us slowly so that we don't break. He expands our vision slowly so that we can take in all of the details of what He desires to accomplish. He causes us to grow slowly so that we stay balanced.

The unfolding of God's plan for your life is a lifelong process. Relax in His presence and allow Him to lead the journey and do His work in you. The Lord will do whatever it takes to prod us toward His higher places. He'll make us restless with where we are if it is time for us to move on. He'll cause us to hunger and thirst for more of Him. He'll plant within us a desire for things that we never dreamed of in our relationship with Him.

Trust God with *all* of the circumstances, relationships, and schedules in your life. Rest in Him. He desires to be your strong and sure haven in all times of frustration.

> Come to Me, all you who labor and are heavy laden, and I will give you rest. Take My yoke upon you and learn from Me, for I am gentle and lowly in heart, and you will find rest for your souls.
>
> —Matthew 11:28-29

☙ What does Jesus mean when He says, "take my yoke upon you"? What does this image of an ox yoke teach you about how to learn from Jesus?

What is the difference between those who "labor" and those who are "heavy laden"? Which type are you?

Peace I leave with you, My peace I give to you; not as the world gives do I give to you. Let not your heart be troubled, neither let it be afraid.

—John 14:27

What sort of peace does the world give? How is this different from the peace that Jesus gives?

☙ Why does Jesus command you not to let your heart be troubled or afraid? What control do you have over these emotions?

─── ☙ **Today and Tomorrow:** ☙ ───

TODAY: LIFE'S FRUSTRATIONS ARE GOD'S WAY OF BUILDING CHRIST-LIKE CHARACTER IN MY LIFE.

TOMORROW: I WILL SPEND TIME IN SCRIPTURES AND PRAYER, SEEKING NOT TO ALLOW MY HEART TO BECOME TROUBLED.

If we choose to,
we're relying
on a falling
world, with
fallen people,
and we will
consiantly let
dan

LESSON 8

Strength in Times of Burnout

---------------- ❧ **In This Lesson:** ☙ ----------------

LEARNING: WHAT IS THE DIFFERENCE BETWEEN SERVING OTHERS AND BURNING MYSELF OUT?

GROWING: WHERE DO I DRAW THE LINE BETWEEN SERVING GOD AND DOING TOO MUCH?

During my years of striving for perfection in my ministry, I knew that I was working too hard for an impossible ideal and that I was expecting too much of myself and others. I justified my behavior, as many perfectionists do, by saying, "God made me this way." The result was that I got on a downward spiral of more and more work in an effort to get better and better and to receive more and more approval. Eventually, I crashed hard.

In 1977, I was doing two 30-minute television programs plus the Sunday morning television program that came from the church, in addition to many other things. I noticed that, instead of just being tired on Monday, I was tired on Tuesday ... and then on Wednesday ... and then all week. I went to the hospital three times that year and had all kinds of tests, and each time the doctors found nothing wrong. I'd promise to take a little break, but it was never a long enough break to really help me. And then the time came when I was so exhausted that I finally took the "orders" of my church board to take a leave of absence for several months. I felt so drained that I wondered if I'd ever regain sufficient strength to function normally.

During the months that followed, I did some serious introspection, and I came to the conclusion that the number-one person who was driving me was *me*. Prior to that time, I would have said that I was doing it all because I loved God. But much of what I was doing for God, I was really doing for myself. Much of my prayer life focused on what I wanted to achieve and on what I wanted to accomplish for the church. I wanted to do it all and have it all. And in the process of pursuing it all, I came to the point of being utterly exhausted physically, mentally, and emotionally.

Have you been in that position? Have you been burned out and then realized that the number-one cause of your burnout was your own unsatisfied ambition? I know many people who have been in this situation.

 When have you experienced burnout—a feeling of total physical, mental, and emotional exhaustion? What did you do? How did the Lord work in your life at that time?

Getting Beyond the Burnout Stage

I took off 12 weeks from the church during this period of burnout. A little to my surprise, I returned to find attendance up, the offering up, and the people happy. God had taken good care of His flock! It took nearly 10 more months, however, for me to feel that I was fully back physically. In the course of those months, I learned several principles that I believe are also reflected in God's Word.

We must learn to rest and to pace ourselves mentally, physically, and emotionally. Mental, physical, and emotional burnout are related. The first step toward being healed of burnout nearly always includes a period of prolonged rest coupled with good nutrition. When you are physically exhausted, your mind and emotions are also affected.

We frequently read in Scripture that Jesus withdrew from His disciples and His ministry to rest and to pray. Here are just a few examples:

ℚ "Jesus withdrew with His disciples to the sea" (Mark 3:7).

ℚ "He Himself often withdrew into the wilderness and prayed" (Luke 5:16).

ℚ "And when He had sent the multitudes away, He went up on the mountain by Himself to pray" (Matthew 14:23).

Six days you shall labor and do all your work, but the seventh day is the Sabbath of the LORD your God. In it you shall do no work.... For in six days the LORD made the heavens and the earth, the sea, and all that is in them, and rested the seventh day. Therefore the LORD blessed the Sabbath day and hallowed it.

—Exodus 20:9-11

According to these verses, why are you commanded to take a day of rest each week? What does this suggest about your *real* motivation in pushing yourself too hard?

What does it mean that God "hallowed" the Sabbath, making it holy? How can a day be holy? How should you *treat* a day that is holy?

We must never get too busy for the basics of our Christian discipline. Loss of Christian disciplines is one of the clearest signs that a person has taken on too much, is involved in too many activities, or is consumed with too many matters. These three basic Christian disciplines are:

1. *Reading God's Word.* Spend time each day in God's Word. What we read becomes part of how we think and respond to life. It becomes our nature, character, attitude, and mind-set.

2. *Spending time in prayer.* Spend time every day talking to God. This is vital if you are to have a walking-and-talking intimacy with the Lord. Spend time telling God how you feel, thank Him for the good things in your life, praise Him for what He has done and for who He is. Share with the Lord your worries, hopes, and desires. Listen for Him to speak His words of comfort, counsel, and direction.

3. *Maintaining fellowship with other believers.* Get involved in a church with those who believe God's Word the way you do. Attend regularly. Volunteer your services in an area where you can share your talents and gifts.

The person who is too busy to attend church, too tired to pray, and too preoccupied to read God's Word has priorities that are out of line and a schedule that is overbooked. Such a person is on his way to burnout.

O God, You are my God; Early will I seek You; My soul thirsts for You; My flesh longs for You in a dry and thirsty land where there is no water. So I have looked for You in the sanctuary, To see Your power and Your glory.

—Psalm 63:1-2

❧ When was the last time that you could honestly tell God that your soul thirsts for Him?

❧ How did David find solace, according to these verses? What can you do to rekindle your desire for God's company?

Make a decision to do only what the Lord requires. Many people reach the burnout stage because they are simply trying to do too many things at the same time. We must keep in mind that God does not commit Himself to helping us do everything that we want to do in our lives. He is committed to helping us do only things *He* wants us to do. God spends His wisdom, knowledge, and understanding on what He wants to see accomplished in your life. Very often, the Lord allows us to reach the burnout stage to teach us His lessons:

❧ That we are doing more than He is requiring us to do

❧ That we have our priorities out of order

❧ That we aren't putting Him first

❧ That we are trying to do too many things at the same time

If you are feeling worn out today, I suggest that you back off from everything and reappraise your life. Make a list of everything that you are doing and identify the time and energy required for each activity. Look for trends and patterns among the activities. Do you find a balance between mental and physical activities? Is there a balance between rest and work? And finally, ask the Lord to reveal to you what it is that is truly important to Him. Ask Him to show you where you need to spend more time, where you need to spend less time, and which activities you might drop. Consider each activity on your list and ask Him, "Is this something that You want me to be doing right now, to this degree and in this way?"

⮞ In the coming week, keep track below (or in a notebook) of all the activities that you are involved in.

With what shall I come before the LORD, And bow myself before the High God? Shall I come before Him with burnt offerings, With calves a year old? Will the LORD be pleased with thousands of rams, Ten thousand rivers of oil? Shall I give my firstborn for my transgression, The fruit of my body for the sin of my soul? He has shown you, O man, what is good; And what does the LORD require of you But to do justly, To love mercy, And to walk humbly with your God?

—Micah 6:6-8

∾ Define the following, giving practical examples of each:

Doing justly

Loving mercy

Walking humbly with God

∾ How do the things listed above compare with your list of activities?

Trust God to help you trust others. One of the most positive lessons that I learned in recuperating from burnout was to yield control over certain activities and responsibilities to others on the church staff. I learned to trust God to give other people both the wisdom and the skill to fill the gaps, and the energy to take up the slack in those areas of authority that I delegated.

To trust others with supervisory or administrative authority, you must first

∽ be willing to share the credit for jobs done well

∽ be willing to let others have relationships which you don't share

∽ be willing to let others make mistakes occasionally rather than to dictate that no mistakes be made

∽ above all, be willing to see others grow in their faith and in their ability to trust God

Jesus Himself is our role model for this. Read in Mark 6:7–9, 12–13 how Jesus sent others into ministry:

> And He called the twelve to Himself, and began to send them out two by two, and gave them power over unclean spirits. He commanded them to take nothing for the journey except a staff—no bag, no bread, no copper in their money belts—but to wear sandals, and not to put on two tunics.... So they went out and preached that people should repent. And they cast out many demons, and anointed with oil many who were sick, and healed them.

✎ Why did Jesus command His disciples "to take nothing for the journey except a staff" (a walking stick)? What does this suggest about your need to prepare for future problems?

✎ What were the results of Jesus delegating the work load to His disciples? How can you delegate some of your work load?

The person who avoids burnout has learned to have:

✎ a balance of rest and work

✎ a balance of mental work and physical work

✎ a good pace to his life

✎ the right priorities of time spent in Bible reading, prayer, and church involvement

✎ trust for others in delegating responsibility

Confront Your Need to Do All and Be All

If you feel driven to do more and more, you must ask yourself, "Why do I have this inner drive to do more than others do?" The answer is going to involve some deep introspection. Most people who have this drive are feeling a lack of God's love in some area of their lives. Any time that we put down our emotional baggage and allow God to invade our memories and our emotional hurts, He will invade our lives with His love.

What a wonderful feeling it is to feel totally accepted and loved by God. That point came fairly late for me in my life, but what a day it was! After that experience, I had no trouble feeling that God loved me. I had no trouble trusting God to be faithful in His love. I had an inner closeness with God unlike any that I had experienced previously, and that closeness has grown to an ever deeper intimacy. Parts of me were healed that I didn't even know were weak or ailing.

I encourage you to come to a point of total surrender of your life, saying to God, "I give everything to You—my life, my relationships, my schedule, my successes and failures, my *all*. I invite You to take over responsibility for my life and to do whatever is necessary to heal me and to give me a deep and abiding sense of Your approval, Your love, and Your presence." God will answer that prayer every time.

> Then Jesus called a little child to Him, set him in the midst of them, and said, "Assuredly, I say to you, unless you are converted and become as little children, you will by no means enter the kingdom of heaven. Therefore whoever humbles himself as this little child is the greatest in the kingdom of heaven."
>
> —Matthew 18:2-4

∞ What does it mean to "become as little children"? How does a child look at life?

∞ What does it mean to humble yourself as a little child? What areas of your life need that sort of humbling this week?

Humble yourselves in the sight of the Lord, and He will lift you up.

—James 4:10

∞ In what ways is being too busy a sign of pride? How can anxiety be a sign of pride?

How will you seek to humble yourself this week?

Today and Tomorrow:

TODAY: SERVING GOD AND OTHERS CAN BECOME AN AREA OF PRIDE, DRAWING ME AWAY FROM GOD.

TOMORROW: THIS WEEK, I WILL ANALYZE MY SCHEDULE AND ASK GOD HOW HE WANTS ME TO SPEND MY TIME.

Notes and Prayer Requests:

Strength in Times of Persecution

---------- ❧ **In This Lesson:** ☙ ----------

LEARNING: WHAT HAPPENS IF I AM PERSECUTED FOR MY FAITH IN GOD?

GROWING: HOW SHOULD I RESPOND TO PEOPLE WHO PERSECUTE ME?

∞

I define persecution as a situation that is abusive and painful, but also a situation in which you know that God wants you to stay and for which there seems to be no human resolution. This is especially true if a person's witness for the Lord is at stake, or if the abuse and pain are being inflicted because your behaviors are based on biblical standards.

I have experienced persecution in my life, and I know that persecution can be intensely hateful and emotionally draining. At one point in my life, I experienced bitter opposition and ungodly assaults for nearly three years without any relief. I forged ahead with what I knew God had called me to do by sheer faith, obedience, and endurance. During that time I became very certain about two truths related to persecution:

1. *God is faithful.* God does not abandon us to persecution; He walks through persecution with us. He never leaves us nor forsakes us. He is with us at all times, and it is His sustaining love and presence that support us in times of persecution.

2. *God will win*. In the end, God has the victory. Whether we live or die in a time of persecution is ultimately unimportant. God's purposes *will* be accomplished on this earth, and we can either have a part in their accomplishment or fail to have a part. The righteous will prevail. God's plan will come to fruition.

You can stake your life on these truths. They can give you the strength to endure whatever persecution comes your way.

> The eyes of the LORD are on the righteous, And His ears are open to their cry. The face of the LORD is against those who do evil, To cut off the remembrance of them from the earth. The righteous cry out, and the LORD hears, And delivers them out of all their troubles. The LORD is near to those who have a broken heart, And saves such as have a contrite spirit.
>
> —Psalms 34:15-18

∼ When have you suffered persecution for doing what was right in God's eyes?

∼ What encouragement can you gain from these verses?

One of the most important things that you can do when persecution strikes is to remind yourself that God is God. He is in control of you and all circumstances. He *will* accomplish all that He desires to accomplish. He is all-knowing, all-powerful, ever-present, everlasting, and always extending an infinite, unconditional love. When persecution comes, make your first thought, *God is in charge! He will be the Victor!*

God Will Deal with His Enemies

Throughout the Scriptures we find many examples of how the Lord deals with His enemies:

    Swiftly. Psalm 64:7 gives us one example, "But God shall shoot at them with an arrow; suddenly they shall be wounded."

    Decisively. Moses told the Israelites, "The Egyptians whom you see today, you shall see again no more forever. The LORD will fight for you, and you shall hold your peace" (Exodus 14:13–14).

    Absolutely. When the sons of Korah rebelled against the commands of the Lord, the earth literally opened and swallowed them up (see Numbers 16).

It is a fearful thing to fight against God, to rebel against God, or to oppose God's people. If you are doing what the Lord has commanded and living in righteousness before the Lord, the enemies who come to persecute you are also making themselves an enemy of God. God defends His people for precisely one reason: they are *His* people.

Now it came to pass, in the morning watch, that the LORD looked down upon the army of the Egyptians through the pillar of fire and cloud, and He troubled the army of the Egyptians. And He took off their chariot wheels, so that they drove them with difficulty; and the Egyptians said, "Let us flee from the face of Israel, for the LORD fights for them against the Egyptians."

—Exodus 14:24-25

∽ Why did God fight against the Egyptians? How did the Egyptians know that it was God they were fighting, and not Israel?

∽ What ultimately became of their army? (See Numbers 14.) How can this encourage you during times of persecution?

How We Deal with Times of Persecution

I believe that there are five vital keys to dealing with persecution.

∽ Keep your eyes on the Lord ∽

Unless you keep your eyes on the Lord, you are likely to find yourself feeling angry, bitter, or resentful against those who are persecuting you. Those emotions can be just as damaging as the persecution itself. Don't compound the problem. Stay focused on Jesus!

Some people consider that all forms of persecution come from the devil. In one regard, they are correct. God never instigates or promotes persecution. On the other hand, God does allow persecution to come our way. We see this clearly in the life of Job. God did not authorize the devil's persecution of Job, but He did allow the devil to test him and to bring situations into his life that might well be described as abusive.

One of His purposes in allowing Job to suffer was to win a battle against the devil. Job's faithfulness and refusal to sin were victories for God over the devil. The Lord also used the devil's persecution in Job's personal life to prepare Job for even greater revelations of Himself.

In nearly every incident of persecution that I've witnessed, I have seen God's purposes at work in much the same way. When a person remains faithful to the Lord and refuses to sin, God gains a victory over the devil—his power is thwarted, his influence is diminished. Plus, a greater strength emerges in the body of Christ, both in the righteous victim and in those who witness the actions of the righteous victim. The victim of persecution who continues to trust in the Lord often has much greater revelations into the Lord's nature, His purposes on this earth, and the relationship that He desires.

Then the LORD said to Satan, "Have you considered My servant Job, that there is none like him on the earth, a blameless and upright man, one who fears God and shuns evil?"

—Job 1:8

∽ Why did God say this to Satan? Why would God allow Satan to persecute His righteous servants?

∽ Read Job 1, and notice that Satan can do nothing without God's permission. What does this teach you about persecution?

∾ **Ask the Lord to sustain you and strengthen you** ∾

The Bible has a great deal to say about those who endure through a period of persecution to emerge victorious on the other side. Even as you pray for the Lord to remove the cause of your persecution, pray for strength to withstand the enemy of your soul until the persecution lifts.

I have fought the good fight, I have finished the race, I have kept the faith. Finally, there is laid up for me the crown of righteousness, which the Lord, the righteous Judge, will give to me on that Day, and not to me only but also to all who have loved His appearing.

—2 Timothy 4:7-8

∾ Consider Paul's three metaphors for persecution: fighting, marathon running, having faith. What insights into perseverance does each of these word pictures suggest?

∾ What does it mean to "love His appearing"? How can that attitude strengthen you in times of persecution?

∾ Recognize that you are fighting a spiritual battle ∾

To be able to withstand persecution, you must know with certainty that the battle is the Lord's—that you are being persecuted for the cause of Christ and not simply for an error or an act of your foolishness or stubbornness. Perhaps the most potent question that you can ask is: "Who will get the glory for a victory?" If the person who is applauded for the victory is anyone other than the Lord Jesus Christ, then mixed motives are in play. To God be the glory for a victory over persecutors and to no one else!

In fighting a spiritual battle, we do well to remind ourselves of Paul's words in Ephesians 6:10–18:

> Be strong in the Lord and in the power of His might. Put on the whole armor of God, that you may be able to stand against the wiles of the devil. For we do not wrestle against flesh and blood, but against principalities, against powers, against the rulers of the darkness of this age, against spiritual hosts of wickedness in the heavenly places. Therefore take up the whole armor of God, that you may be able to withstand in the evil day, and having done all, to stand. Stand therefore, having girded your waist with truth, having put on the breastplate of righteousness, and having shod your feet with the preparation of the gospel of peace; above all, taking the shield of faith with which you will be able to quench all the fiery darts of the wicked one. And take the helmet of salvation, and the sword of the Spirit, which is the word of God; praying always with all prayer and supplication in the Spirit, being watchful to this end with all perseverance and supplication for all the saints.

℞ Consider each of these pieces of armor. How is each used? What does each do?

Belt (of truth)

Breastplate (of righteousness)

Boots (of the gospel)

Shield (of faith)

Helmet (of salvation)

Sword (of the Spirit)

℞ Now consider the spiritual application for each piece of armor. How is "truth" like a belt, and so forth?

What you arm yourself with in times of persecution is especially important.

🕭 *Arm yourself with the truth.* Make sure that you know the truth of the situation from God's perspective.

🕭 *Arm yourself with righteousness.* Make certain that you are in right standing with God and that you are living a blameless life before your persecutors. Persecution gives you no license to sin.

🕭 *Arm yourself with God's peace.* Make peace your goal—true reconciliation, not merely a truce.

🕭 *Arm yourself with faith.* Keep your focus on Jesus.

🕭 *Arm yourself with the confidence of your salvation and deliverance at God's hand.* Expect the victory to come!

🕭 *Arm yourself with the Word of God.* Be quick to speak the Word of God in the midst of your persecution. Let God's Word do your talking for you.

🕭 *Endure in prayer.* Pray for those who are persecuting you. Pray for God to save them. Pray for your fellow believers, that God will strengthen them as they stand with you in your time of persecution.

🕭 *Persevere.* Don't give up. Don't give in. Remain solidly grounded in the Lord and *stand.*

⟅ Treat your persecutors with godly love and kindness ⟆

Our first impulse is nearly always to respond to persecution with equal force—to retaliate, to fight, to go on the offensive even as we build a strong defense against our persecutors. The Bible presents a very different course of action to us. Jesus taught that we are to treat our persecutors with kindness—speaking well of them, praying for them, and responding to them with godly love. This is tough to do, but this is what we are commanded by the Lord to do!

Jesus also taught that we are to turn the other cheek to those who strike us, that we are to "give" in times of persecution, rather than to withdraw or to wither into silent submission. In many ways, giving is a very strong action during persecution. Giving and showing kindness foil the attempts of persecutors. The anger and hatred felt by a persecutor can't help but be thwarted when faced with a loving, giving, praying victim. Ask the Lord to give you the strength to become an active *giver* in times of persecution, not only an enduring saint.

> "But I say to you who hear: Love your enemies, do good to those who hate you, bless those who curse you, and pray for those who spitefully use you. To him who strikes you on the one cheek, offer the other also. And from him who takes away your cloak, do not withhold your tunic either. Give to everyone who asks of you. And from him who takes away your goods do not ask them back."

—Luke 6:27-30

 When have you responded to persecution with a counter-attack? When have you responded with kindness? What were the results of each?

 Notice that the Lord commands that we do more than simply endure persecution; He calls us to actively return love and kindness in response to hatred. What does this teach us about the love of God?

∞ Look for the victory ∞

Never lose sight of the goal, the reason for the pain and rejection that you may be experiencing. Jesus taught:

> Blessed are those who are persecuted for righteousness' sake,
> For theirs is the kingdom of heaven. Blessed are you when they revile and persecute you, and say all kinds of evil against you falsely for My sake. Rejoice and be exceedingly glad, for great is your reward in heaven.
>
> —Matthew 5:10–12

The kingdom of heaven is to be gained through your persecution. Not only that, but a great reward within the kingdom of heaven is yours. There's no comparison between the earthly, transient anger of persecutors and the glory of eternity. Always keep in mind that persecution is only for a season. As painful as it may be, all persecution is temporary. Eternity awaits!

Look, too, for the victory that will come in your own life. Your faith will be strengthened, you will gain a greater resolve to win souls, your character will be refined, and you will have greater cause to praise God. Expect the clouds to lift and the glory of God to be revealed when your time of persecution is over!

> But hold fast what you have till I come. And he who overcomes, and keeps My works until the end, to him I will give power over the nations.
>
> —Revelation 2:25-26

List below as many Bible characters as you can who suffered persecution for God. How long did they have to endure persecution? How long have they been enjoying the glory of God's presence?

What is the very worst thing that you could lose in a time of persecution? What is the very least that you will gain for eternity?

"But if you love those who love you, what credit is that to you? For even sinners love those who love them. And if you do good to those who do good to you, what credit is that to you? For even sinners do the same. And if you lend to those from whom you hope to receive back, what credit is that to you? For even sinners lend to sinners to receive as much back. But love your enemies, do good, and lend, hoping for nothing in return; and your reward will be great, and you will be sons of the Most High. For He is kind to the unthankful and evil."

—Luke 6:32-35

➣ What is to be our motivation in showing love to those who hate us, according to these verses?

➣ According to these verses, why should we rejoice during times of persecution?

❧ Today and Tomorrow: ❧

TODAY: I NEED TO REMEMBER THAT I AM IN A SPIRITUAL BATTLE AGAINST THE FORCES OF DARKNESS.

TOMORROW: I WILL CONSIDER ALL ELEMENTS OF THE ARMOR OF GOD, AND WILL WORK ON ARMING MYSELF THIS WEEK.

❧ Notes and Prayer Requests: ❧

Lesson 10

Strength in Times of Brokenness

┌─────────── ☙ In This Lesson: ❧ ───────────┐

LEARNING: WHY HAS MY LIFE FALLEN APART?

GROWING: WHAT CAN I POSSIBLY GAIN FROM BEING BROKEN?

└──────────────── ∞ ────────────────┘

We all know what it means to be broken—to feel shattered or blown apart, as if our entire world has fallen apart. We all have times when we don't want to raise our head off the pillow and when we feel certain that the tears will never stop flowing. Brokenness is often accompanied by emptiness—a void that cannot be filled, sorrow that cannot be comforted, a wound for which there is no balm.

The most painful and difficult times of my life have been those times when I felt broken. I don't like pain, suffering, or feelings of brokenness any more than anybody else does. Certain circumstances in my life have *hurt*, at times so intensely that I thought I might never heal. But one of the things that I have discovered through being broken is that, *after* brokenness, we are very likely to experience God's greatest presence. After brokenness, our lives can be more fruitful, more purposeful, and more joyful. A genuine blessing can come in the wake of being broken.

One of the greatest examples of brokenness that we have in the Bible is that of Peter, and perhaps the most famous scene in Peter's life happened the night before Jesus was crucified. Jesus was arrested in the Garden of Gethsemane, and Peter followed at a distance to the place where He was taken. As Peter sat in the courtyard of the high priest's house, a servant girl looked closely at him and said, "This man was with Jesus." Peter denied knowing Jesus.

A little while later, someone else saw him and said, "You are one of them." Again, Peter denied the association. A while later, yet another person said, "He was with Him." Peter said, "I don't know what you're talking about." And at that moment, Peter came to the full realization that he had disowned Jesus in fear when questioned by a few lowly servants. Peter no doubt felt broken in that moment, shattered before God and before the mirror of his own soul.

Peter was talented and gifted in many ways. He was impulsive, strong-willed, outspoken, and strong physically. He was also self-centered. Yet Jesus chose Peter. Why? For the same reason that He chooses us: Jesus sees all that we *can* be. For us to become all that we can be, however, we must experience a "breaking"—a sanding, a sifting, a chiseling of our souls so that we truly begin to be conformed to the likeness of Jesus Christ. That's what happened to Peter, and it's what happens to each one of us.

✎ When have you experienced times of brokenness? What did you do? What was the outcome?

~ What blessings have you seen in your own life as a result of times of being broken?

Three Aspects of the Breaking Process

There are three aspects to God's breaking process. We see them in the life of Peter, but also in our own lives.

∞ God targets the area that needs to be broken ∞

Each of us has strengths and weaknesses, attitudes, habits, relationships, and desires. God knows the specific areas that need to be refashioned and brought to a point of greater maturity. The Lord knew that Peter's impetuous, volatile nature—subject to intense faith one moment and intense fear the next—needed to be refashioned. We see how the Lord dealt with this in Matthew 14.

Jesus came walking on the water to His disciples, who had been struggling against wind and stormy waters. The Lord called out to them, "Be of good cheer! It is I; do not be afraid." Peter answered by saying, "Lord, if it is You, command me to come to You on the water." And Jesus said, "Come." But then when Peter had gone out of the boat and walked on the water, he got his eyes off Jesus and onto the wind. He was afraid and began to sink, crying out, "Lord, save me!" Jesus stretched out His hand and caught him and said, "O you of little faith, why did you doubt?" Together they got into the boat and the wind ceased (see

116

Matthew 14:27–31). Peter needed to be challenged, even "broken" in this area of his life so that he might not vacillate between faith and fear, but stand strong in faith.

The good news of the Scriptures is that God created us and He knows us. He knows us as we are right now, and He knows who we *can* be, what we *can* do, and what He has fashioned and formed us to do. In times of brokenness, trust that God is doing something in you for your eternal good and for the fulfillment of His plan and purpose in your life. God has not abandoned you in brokenness—rather, He is working during this time and in this situation to create in you something good.

> "Before I formed you in the womb I knew you; Before you were born I sanctified you; I ordained you a prophet to the nations."

> —Jeremiah 1:5

꙾ According to these verses, who designed the person that you are?

꙾ What "rough edges" is God sanding off your character? How can you help Him to speed the process?

∞ God chooses the tools of our brokenness ∞

Why did Jesus walk on water to His disciples? In part, He was setting up the situation in which He could teach Peter and the other disciples. God always brings about the circumstances of our breaking in two ways. At times, He engineers the situation that will cause us to confront what He desires to change in us. At other times, God will simply allow us to follow the path of sin and error that we have chosen. He will give us enough rope so we can entangle ourselves.

God also chooses the tools to break us. He allows us to confront the hurtful remarks or false accusations of people, erroneous negative reports, or people who attempt to manipulate us for their own purposes. He chooses the methods, sometimes even allowing our enemies to be tools in His hands.

What we must realize in times of brokenness is that God's methods are not always going to be readily understood by us. In fact, most of the time God's ways will confound us—He often chooses the very opposite of what *we* would choose as a tool with which to work for our good.

> "For My thoughts are not your thoughts, Nor are your ways My ways," says the LORD. "For as the heavens are higher than the earth, So are My ways higher than your ways, And My thoughts than your thoughts."
>
> —Isaiah 55:8-9

∞ What does it mean that God's ways are "higher" than our ways? What does this have to do with being broken?

∽ What is God's most important "thought" or goal for your life? How have you seen Him gradually working that out in the past?

∽ God controls the pressure in our brokenness ∽

God sets limits on our brokenness—limits on how long the brokenness continues and on the amount of pain and suffering that we experience. God limits the amount of hurting that He allows us to do. What might we do to hasten the end of a period of brokenness?

First, brokenness ends when we yield to God in submission. The moment that we surrender completely to God, God begins to reverse the circumstances related to our brokenness and to remove the tools that He has used in the breaking process.

Second, brokenness ends when it reaches such an intensity that it will damage God's purpose for your life. God will not allow you to be broken to the point where you cannot engage in the ministry that He has prepared for you. His purpose is to train you, refashion you, mold you, conform you to Christ's image—not to destroy you.

When you begin to experience a time of brokenness, yield quickly to the Lord. Ask Him what He is seeking to accomplish in your life, and become willing to do what God is asking, change what God is seeking to change, or embark on what God is calling you to do. Just as Jesus prayed in the Garden of Gethsemane, we must reach the point where we say, "Not my will, but Your will, God."

Cause me to hear Your lovingkindness in the morning, For in You do I trust; Cause me to know the way in which I should walk, For I lift up my soul to You.

—Psalms 143:8

☙ What must you do first if you want to "hear" God? What is the first step in "knowing" anything?

☙ If God shows you "the way in which you should walk", what will He require from you as a result?

Restoration After Brokenness

Once we yield ourselves to the goals that the Lord is seeking to accomplish in our lives, the Lord often reveals Himself to us in extremely loving and tender ways. This happened in the life of Peter. After the crucifixion of Jesus, Peter returned to fishing. Jesus found him by the seashore one morning, and He said to him, "Peter, do you love Me?" Three times Jesus asked this question, and three times Peter said, "Lord, You know I do!"

Jesus restored Peter to a relationship with Himself. He forgave him fully for his denial: three times, Peter denied knowing Jesus, and three times, Peter had the opportunity to affirm his love for the Lord. And then, Jesus gave him something to do: to feed and care for "the sheep"— the followers of Jesus who were in need of a leader. Peter finally yielded fully to the Lord's will. The Lord gave him a supernatural ministry, one that was realized in a powerful way beginning on the day of Pentecost. (See Peter's powerful sermon in Acts 2.)

The Lord's purpose in brokenness may have many facets to it, but one thing will always result: a greater opportunity for ministry to others. In the aftermath of your pain, the Lord will give you opportunities to minister to others who are going through a similar experience. Your time of brokenness prepares you for a time of greater fruitfulness in your ministry.

Brokenness is a pruning process. Jesus taught, "Every branch in Me that does not bear fruit He takes away; and every branch that bears fruit He prunes, that it may bear more fruit" (John 15:2). If you truly are going to be fruitful in the Lord's kingdom, you *will* experience a pruning process, a refining process. The end result will be for your good, and for the good of others and the expansion of the Lord's kingdom.

> "I am the true vine, and My Father is the vinedresser. Every branch in Me that does not bear fruit He takes away; and every branch that bears fruit He prunes, that it may bear more fruit."
>
> —John 15:1-2

❧ What is involved in pruning a tree or bush? How does this apply to spiritual pruning?

❧ In what area of your life would you like to be more "fruitful"? What might God have to prune away to accomplish that?

The Blessings from Brokenness

At least five blessings come from our being broken before the Lord:

1. *We understand God better.* We come into a greater understanding of the absolutes of God—that His commandments are exact, His promises are sure, and His methods and timetable are His own. We understand the Scriptures more fully . We come to a greater understanding of all of God's attributes.

2. *We understand ourselves better.* When we are broken, we understand more about our own inner motivations, desires, and weaknesses. Very often, we experience an opportunity to ask God's forgiveness in areas of life that we had not thought to confront. We can be freed from confusion about our own past, and God can heal old emotional wounds.

3. *We have increased compassion for others.* Usually when a person gains new insight into himself through brokenness, he emerges with a greater empathy for others and a greater compassion for those who are hurting. Brokenness makes us less critical and judgmental.

4. *We have a greater enthusiasm for life.* When we come to the end of ourselves and stand on the brink of God's unconditional love, we find that we have a greater appreciation for all of God's gifts to us. Life takes on a new zest. We often find that we are more creative and more willing to express ourselves. We have a greater ability to enjoy those things that amount to good, clean fun.

5. *We have an increased awareness of God's presence.* God is with us always, but brokenness often makes us more keenly aware of His presence and more sensitive to His desires. In feeling God's presence with us, we have a greater feeling of security.

Is brokenness worth the pain and struggle? With blessings such as these, we can say with joy as we look back on a period of brokenness, "I am grateful for all that I've been through." The key, however, is in turning to the Lord in our brokenness. Those who turn to any other person or thing, or seek to escape their brokenness, find themselves experiencing only more of the same—and often even greater pain, discouragement, or despair. Trust God, and God alone, to do *His* work in you in times when you feel shattered and broken. Allow Him to put you back together in *His* way, in *His* timing, and for *His* purposes.

"I will bring the one-third through the fire, Will refine them as silver is refined, And test them as gold is tested. They will call on My name, And I will answer them. I will say, 'This is My people'; And each one will say, 'The LORD is my God.'"

—Zechariah 13:9

🐦 Why is silver refined? How is it done?

🐦 What areas of your own life still need to be refined? How can you help God in that process?

🐦 Today and Tomorrow: 🐦

TODAY: GOD USES THE BREAKING PROCESS, LIKE THE PRUNING PROCESS, TO MAKE ME MORE LIKE JESUS.

TOMORROW: I WILL ASK THE LORD TO SHOW ME AREAS THAT NEED HIS PRUNING, AND I WILL SUBMIT TO HIS HAND.

11169754R0

Made in the USA
Lexington, KY
14 September 2011